THE BEST

CATHOLIC
2006
WRITING

D1319139

THE BEST

CATHOLIC

2006

WRITING

EDITED BY

BRIAN DOYLE

LOYOLAPRESS.
CHICAGO

LOYOLA PRESS.

3441 N. ASHLAND AVENUE
CHICAGO, ILLINOIS 60657
(800) 621-1008
WWW.LOYOLABOOKS.ORG

Cover and interior design by Think Design Group

ISBN 0-8294-2356-7
International Standard Serial Number (ISSN) 1556-259X

Printed in the United States of America
06 07 08 09 10 11 Versa 10 9 8 7 6 5 4 3 2 1

For Cynthia Ozick, whose prose is prayer

Contents

Introduction

A while ago I was shuffling along the roaring shore of the misnamed Pacific Ocean, humming to myself, pondering this and that and tother, when I saw a crippled kid hopping toward me. She was maybe four years old and her feet were bent so sideways that her toes faced each other, so she scuttled rather than walked. I never saw a kid crippled quite like that before. I thought for a minute she was alone but then I noticed the rest of her clan, a big guy and two other small girls, probably the dad and sisters, walking way ahead.

The crippled kid was cheerful as a bird and she zoomed along awfully fast on those sideways feet. She was totally absorbed in the sea wrack at the high-tide line—shards of crab and acres of sand fleas and shreds of seaweed and ropes of bullwhip kelp and fractions of jellyfish and here and there a deceased perch or auklet or cormorant or gull, and once a serious-size former fish that looked like it might have been a salmon. In the way of all people for a million years along all shores she stared and poked and prodded and bent and pocketed and discarded, pawing through the loot and litter of the merciless musing sea.

She was so into checking out tide treasure that her dad and sisters got way out ahead of her. After a while the dad turned and whistled and the crippled kid looked up and laughed and took off hopping faster than you could ever imagine a kid that crippled could hop, and when she was a few feet away from the dad he crouched a little and extended his arm behind him with his hand out to receive her foot, and she shinnied up his arm as graceful and quick as anything you ever saw.

She slid into what must have been her usual seat on his neck and off they went, the sisters moaning about having to wait for the crippled kid and the dad tickling the bottoms of the kid's feet, so that I heard the kid laughing fainter and fainter as they receded, until finally I couldn't hear her laughing anymore. But right about then I was weeping like a child anyways, at the intricate astounding unimaginable inexplicable complex thicket of love and pain and suffering and joy, at the way that kid rocketed up her daddy's arm quick as a cat, at the way he crouched just so and opened his palm so his baby girl could come flying up the holy branch of his arm, at the way her hands knew where to wrap themselves around his grin, at the way the sisters grumbled about their kid sister but would pound silly anyone else who ever grumbled about her.

And this is all not even to mention the glory of the sunlight that day, and the basso moan of mother sea, and the deft diving of the little black sea-ducks in the surf, and the seal popping up here and there looking eerily like my grandfather, and the eagle who flew over like a black tent heading north, and the extraordinary fact that the Coherent Mercy granted me my own kids, who were not crippled, and were at that exact moment arguing shrilly about baseball at the other end of the beach.

I finally got a grip and set to shuffling again, but that kid stays with me. Something about her, the way she was a verb, the way she was happy even with the dark cards she was dealt, the way she loved openly and artlessly, the way even her sisters couldn't stay pissy but had to smile when she shinnied up their daddy's arm, seems utterly holy to me, a gift, a sign, a reminder, a letter from the Lord.

In my Father's house are many mansions, said the thin confusing peripatetic rabbi long ago, a line I have always puzzled over, yet another of the man's many Zen koans, but I think I finally have a handle on that one. What he meant, did Yesuah ben Joseph of the haunting life and message, is that we are given gifts beyond measure, beyond price, beyond understanding, and they mill and swirl by us all day and night, and we have but to see them clearly, for a second, to believe wholly in the bounty and generosity and mercy of *I Am Who Am.*

I am not stupid, at least not all the time, and I saw how crippled that kid was, and I can only imagine her life to date and to come, and the tensions and travails of her family, and the battles she will fight and the tears she will shed, and I see and hear the roar of pain and suffering in the world, the floods and rapes and starvings and bullets, and I am too old and too honest not to admit how murderous and greedy we can be.

But I have also seen too many kids who are verbs to not believe we swim in an ocean of holy. I have seen so many men and women and children of such grace and humor and mercy that I know I have seen the Christ ten times a day. I think maybe you know that too and we just don't talk about it much because we are tired and scared and the light flits in and around so much darkness. But there was a crippled kid on the beach and the Christ in her came pouring out her eyes and I don't forget it.

In my Father's house are many mansions, said the Christos, confusingly, and then in his usual testy editorial way, *if it were not so, I would have told you,* and then, in a phrase I lean on when things go dark, *I go to prepare a place for you.*

But we are already in the doorway of the house, don't you think?

—Brian Doyle

A Note on the Selections

It's three years down the road now from the first volume of Loyola Press's annual Best Catholic Writing anthology, which was hatched in the sunny opening stanzas of 2003, and they have been a wild three years. I think I have read a couple thousand articles and essays and stories and poems and blogs, and my eyes are shot, and the recycling guy is exhausted, and if I ever hear the words *Mel Gibson* and *Passion* in the same sentence again I will scream. On the other hand, the editors at Loyola Press and I have discovered that what we had hoped deep in our hearts is true: there's a *stunning* amount of terrific Catholic writing—writing that is by Catholics or about Catholics, writing that grapples with the essence of the Catholic idea—being committed every year. There's a startling number of voices, very many of them honest, eloquent, angry, and hilarious. So it's been a great deal of fun to try to catch some of them in these pages.

It's also awful tiring, and I am older than dirt now, and I really want to write bad novels, which are the only kind that ever make money and then are made into movies where the *real* money is, and I have three kids, so it's either writing for the movies or being a plumber when it comes to making serious cash, and I can't plumb. So I am formally handing the editor's tiara to Loyola Press's Jim Manney, who has been actively involved in editing these collections all along. I'm going to stay involved in this project as an editor. But henceforth e-mail Jim at manney@loyolapress.com with your candidates for the tome. Not me. He likes e-mail, and he is at Loyola Press, 3441 North Ashland Avenue, Chicago, IL 60657, if you prefer paper mail.

We are often asked how we pick pieces for the Best Catholic Writing anthology. Answer: we read everything we can get our hands on—magazines, newspapers, newsletters, blogs, speeches, webzines, scripts, transcripts, songs, books, manuscripts, etc. Writers send stuff, as do publishers, editors, monks, poets, plumbers—everyone. And that's great, for though we try hard to scour for anything that has bone and poetry and passion in it, there's a vast universe out there.

Send all this to Jim Manney. As the late great Polish pope said, be not afraid. Send whatever you think might fit—anything that sparked your heart when you read it. Jim reads fast.

We have also often been asked what the criteria are by which a piece is chosen for the anthology. Answer: I can't explain it very well. Generally the pieces with the best chance of being selected are those that are not stuffy, enormous, political, or devout with a capital *D*. The only thing I can say easily is that the best pieces are *real*—real stories, real emotions and opinions, real maps of the heart.

I should note that we cheerfully read and sometimes accept pieces from all nations (see George Coyne's piece on evolution from the British journal *The Tablet*); that the very biggest and most controversial subjects are of course meat for this maw (see the essay about torture by the wonderful Australian writer Martin Flanagan in this edition); and that we are fascinated by all forms of storytelling (blogs, it turns out, are a really interesting form of writing, or ranting; see the testy string of bloggery in this edition).

I should also note here that while it is a venial sin to include an essay of your own in a collection you are editing, the piece here about a very brave man named Eddy wasn't written by me so much as it was told, hauntingly, to me, so I figure I am absolved.

It has been my conviction, during these first three years, that *Catholic* absolutely means catholic. Yes, of course, we are interested in pieces by, for, and about Catholics. But it would be a poor church that did not seek to grapple with good and evil and grace and greed and courage and cruelty and prayer and passion and sensuality and commerce and war and God on the largest possible scale. This anthology does that. Yes, you bet we are interested in pieces by, for, and about Buddhists, agnostics, and even Yankees fans.

A last note: prayers all around. Every act, every thought, every lurch toward the extraordinary grace of our best selves is a prayer of astounding possible power and poetry. I wish headlong lurching for us all.

—Brian Doyle

We Want God

Peggy Noonan

from *The Wall Street Journal*

When John Paul II went to Poland, communism didn't have a prayer.

Everyone speaks of John Paul II's role in the defeat of Soviet communism and the liberation of Eastern Europe. We don't know everything, or even a lot, about the quiet diplomatic moves—what happened in private, what kind of communications the pope had with the other great lions of the 1980s, Reagan and Thatcher, and others, including Bill Casey, the tough old fox of the CIA, and Lech Walesa of Solidarity.

But I think I know the moment Soviet communism began its fall. It happened in public. Anyone could see it. It was one of the great spiritual moments of the twentieth century, maybe the greatest.

It was the first week in June 1979. Europe was split in two between East and West, the democracies and the communist bloc—police states controlled by the Soviet Union and run by local communist parties and secret police.

John Paul was a new pope, raised to the papacy just eight months before.

The day after he became pope he made it clear he would like to return as pope to his native Poland to see his people. The Communists who ran the Polish regime faced a quandary. If they didn't allow the new pope to return to his homeland, they would look defensive and frightened, as if they feared that he had more power than they. To rebuff him would seem an admission of their weakness. On the other hand, if they let him return, the people might rise up against the government, which might in turn trigger an invasion by the Soviet Union.

The Polish government decided that it would be too great an embarrassment to refuse the pope. So they invited him, gambling that John Paul—whom they knew when he was cardinal of Kraków, who they were sure would not want his presence to inspire bloodshed—would be prudent. They wagered that he would understand he was fortunate to be given permission to come, that he would understand what he owed the government in turn was deportment that would not threaten the reigning reality. They announced the pope would be welcome to come home on a "religious pilgrimage."

John Paul quickly accepted the invitation. He went to Poland.

And from the day he arrived, the boundaries of the world began to shift.

Two months before the pope's arrival, the Polish communist apparatus took steps to restrain the enthusiasm of the people. They sent a secret directive to schoolteachers explaining how they should understand and explain the pope's visit. "The pope is our enemy," it said.

Due to his uncommon skills and great sense of humor he is dangerous, because he charms everyone, especially journalists. Besides, he goes for cheap gestures in his relations with the crowd, for instance, puts on a highlander's hat, shakes all hands, kisses children. . . . It is modeled on American presidential campaigns. . . . Because of the activities of the Church in Poland our activities designed to atheize the youth not only cannot diminish but must intensely develop. . . . In this respect all means are allowed and we cannot afford any sentiments.

The government also issued instructions to Polish media to censor and limit the pope's comments and appearances.

On June 2, 1979, the pope arrived in Poland. What followed will never be forgotten by those who witnessed it.

He knelt and kissed the ground, the dull gray tarmac of the airport outside Warsaw. The silent churches of Poland at that moment began to ring their bells. The pope traveled by motorcade from the airport to the Old City of Warsaw.

The government had feared hundreds or thousands or even tens of thousands would line the streets and highways.

By the end of the day, with the people lining the streets and highways plus the people massed outside Warsaw and then inside it—all of them cheering and throwing flowers and applauding and singing—more than a million had come.

In Victory Square in the Old City the pope gave a Mass. Communist officials watched from the windows of nearby hotels. The pope gave what papal biographer George Weigel called the greatest sermon of John Paul's life.

Why, the pope asked, had God lifted a Pole to the papacy? Perhaps it was because of how Poland had suffered for centuries, and through the twentieth century had become "the land of a particularly responsible witness" to God. The people of Poland, he suggested, had been chosen for a great role: to understand, humbly but surely, that they were the repository of a special "witness of his cross and his resurrection." He asked then if the people of Poland accepted the obligations of such a role in history.

The crowd responded with thunder.

"We want God!" they shouted. "We want God!"

What a moment in modern history: *We want God.* From the mouths of modern men and women living in a modern atheistic dictatorship.

The pope was speaking on the vigil of Pentecost, that moment in the New Testament when the Holy Spirit came down to Christ's apostles, who had been hiding in fear after his crucifixion, filling them with courage and joy. John Paul picked up this theme. What was the greatest of the works of God? Man. Who redeemed man? Christ. Therefore, he declared, "Christ cannot be kept out of the history of man in any part of the globe, at any longitude or latitude. . . . The exclusion of Christ from the history of man is an act against man! Without Christ it is impossible to understand the history of Poland." Those who oppose Christ, he said, still live within the Christian context of history.

Christ, the pope declared, was not only the past of Poland—he was also "the future . . . our Polish future."

The massed crowd thundered its response. "We want God!" it roared.

That is what the communist apparatchiks watching the Mass from the hotels that rimmed Victory Square heard. Perhaps at this point they understood that they had made a strategic mistake. Perhaps as John Paul spoke they heard the sound careen off the hard buildings that ringed the square; perhaps the echo sounded like a wall falling.

The pope had not directly challenged the government. He had not called for an uprising. He had not told the people of Catholic Poland to push back against their atheist masters. He simply stated the obvious. In Mr. Weigel's words, "Poland was not a communist country; Poland was a Catholic nation saddled with a communist state."

The next day, June 3, 1979, John Paul stood outside the cathedral in Gniezno, a small city with a population of fifty thousand or so. Again there was an outdoor Mass, and again he said an amazing thing.

He did not speak of what governments want, or directly of what a growing freedom movement wants.

He spoke of what God wants.

"Does not Christ want, does not the Holy Spirit demand, that the pope, himself a Pole, the pope, himself a Slav, here and now should bring out into the open the spiritual unity of Christian Europe?" Yes, he said, Christ wants that. "The Holy Spirit demands that it be said aloud, here, now. . . . Your countryman comes to you, the pope, so as to speak before the whole church, Europe, and the world. . . . He comes to cry out with a mighty cry."

What John Paul was saying was remarkable. He was telling Poland: See the reality around you differently. See your situation in a new way. Do not see the division of Europe; see the wholeness that exists and that not even communism can take away. Rhetorically his approach was not to declare or assert but merely, again, to point out the obvious: We are Christians, we are here, we are united, no matter what the Communists and their mapmakers say.

It was startling. It was as if he were talking about a way of seeing the secret order of the world.

That day at the cathedral the communist authorities could not stop the applause. They could not stop everyone who applauded and cheered. There weren't enough jail cells.

But it was in the Blonie field, in Kraków—the Blonia Krakówskie, the field on the outskirts of the city—that the great transcendent moment of the pope's trip took place. It was the moment when, for those looking back, the new world opened. It was the moment, some said later, that Soviet communism's fall became inevitable.

It was a week into the trip, June 10, 1979. It was a sunny day. The pope was to hold a public Mass. The communist government had not allowed it to be publicized, but Poles had spread the word.

Government officials braced themselves, because now they knew a lot of people might come, as they had to John Paul's first Mass. But that was a week before. Since then, maybe people had seen enough of him. Maybe they were tiring of his message. Maybe it wouldn't be so bad.

But something happened in the Blonie field.

They started coming early, and by the time the Mass began it was the biggest gathering of humanity in the entire history of Poland. Two million or three million people came—no one is sure. Maybe more. For a Mass.

And it was there, at the end of his trip, in the Blonie field, that John Paul took on communism directly, by focusing on communism's attempt to kill the religious heritage of a country that had for a thousand years believed in Christ.

This is what he said:

> Is it possible to dismiss Christ and everything which he brought into the annals of the human being? Of course it is possible. The human

being is free. The human being can say to God, "No." The human being can say to Christ, "No." But the critical question is: Should he? And in the name of what "should" he? With what argument, what reasoning, what value held by the will or the heart does one bring oneself, one's loved ones, one's countrymen and nation to reject, to say "no" to him with whom we have all lived for one thousand years? He who formed the basis of our identity and has himself remained its basis ever since. . . .

As a bishop does in the sacrament of confirmation, so do I today extend my hands in that apostolic gesture over all who are gathered here today, my compatriots. And so I speak for Christ himself: "Receive the Holy Spirit!"

I speak too for St. Paul: "Do not quench the Spirit!"

I speak again for St. Paul: "Do not grieve the spirit of God!"

You must be strong, my brothers and sisters! You must be strong with the strength that faith gives! You must be strong with the strength of faith! You must be faithful! You need this strength today more than any other period of our history. . . .

You must be strong with love, which is stronger than death. . . . When we are strong with the spirit of God, we are also strong with the faith of man. . . . . There is therefore no need to fear. . . . So . . . I beg you: never lose your trust, do not be defeated, do not be discouraged. . . . Always seek spiritual power from him from whom countless generations of our fathers and mothers have found it. Never detach yourselves from him. Never lose your spiritual freedom.

They went home from that field a changed country. After that Mass they would never be the same.

What John Paul did in the Blonie field was both a departure from his original comments in Poland and an extension of them.

In his first comments he said: God sees one unity of Europe; he does not see East and West divided by a gash in the soil.

In this way he divided the dividers from God's view of history.

But in the Blonie field he extended his message. He called down the Holy Spirit—as the Vicar of Christ and successor to Peter, he called down God—to fill the people of Poland, to "confirm" their place in history and their ancient choice of Christ, to confirm, as it were, that their history was real and right and unchangeable—even unchangeable by Communists.

So it was a redeclaration of the Polish spirit, which is a free spirit. And those who were there went home a different people, a people who saw themselves differently, not as victims of history but as strugglers for Christ.

Another crucial thing happened, after the Mass was over. Everyone who was there went home and turned on the news that night to see the pictures of the incredible crowd and the incredible pope. But state-controlled TV did not show the crowds. They did a brief report that showed a shot of the pope standing and speaking for a second or two. State television did not acknowledge or admit what a phenomenon John Paul's visit was, or what it had unleashed.

The people who had been at the Mass could compare the reality their own eyes had witnessed with the propaganda their media reported. They could see the discrepancy. This left the people of Poland able to say at once and together, definitively, with no room for argument: It's all lies. Everything this government says is a lie. Everything it *is* is a lie.

Whatever legitimacy the government could pretend to, it began to lose. One by one the people of Poland said to themselves, or for themselves within themselves: It is over.

And when ten million Poles said that to themselves, it was over in Poland. And when it was over in Poland, it was over in Eastern Europe. And when it was over in Eastern Europe, it was over in the Soviet Union. And when it was over in the Soviet Union, well, it was over.

All of this was summed up by a Polish publisher and intellectual named Jerzy Turowicz, who had known Karol Wojtyla when they were young men together, and who had gone on to be a supporter of Solidarity and a member of Poland's first postcommunist government. Mr. Turowicz, remembering the Blonie field and the pope's visit, told Ray Flynn, at the time U.S. ambassador to the Vatican, "Historians say World War II ended in 1945. Maybe in the rest of the world, but not in Poland. They say communism fell in 1989. Not in Poland. World War II and communism both ended in Poland at the same time—in 1979, when John Paul II came home."

And now he is dead. It is fitting and not at all surprising that Rome, to its shock, was overwhelmed with millions of people come to see him for the last time. The line to view his body in St. Peter's stretched more than a mile. His funeral was witnessed by an estimated one billion people, the biggest television event in history. And no one, in Poland or elsewhere, could edit the tape to hide what was happening.

John Paul gave us what may be the transcendent public spiritual moment of the twentieth century: "We want God." The greatest and most authentic cry of the human heart.

They say he asked that his heart be removed from his body and buried in Poland. That sounds right, and I hope it's true. They'd better get a big box.

Five Years with Dorothy Day

Robert Ellsberg

from *America*

She believed that in each situation, in each encounter, there is a path to God.

I met Dorothy Day in the fall of 1975, when I was nineteen. I had taken an undergraduate leave of absence from Harvard University and made my way to the Catholic Worker headquarters in New York City, drawn by a number of motivations. I was eager to learn something directly about life, apart from books. I was tired of living for myself alone and longed to give myself to something larger and more meaningful. But mostly, I think, I was drawn by the hope of meeting Dorothy Day, the movement's legendary founder and still, at seventy-seven, editor of its newspaper. I had planned to stay a few months, but I was pretty quickly hooked and remained for five years—the last five years of Dorothy's life, as it turned out.

Our first meeting occurred on the first floor of St. Joseph's House, the large room that served as soup kitchen, meeting hall, or chapel, depending on the occasion. Dorothy, who dressed in donated clothes, took pride in the times when she was mistaken for one of the homeless women on the Bowery. But there was no mistaking the authority she carried, even among the down-and-out characters who made up the Catholic Worker family.

To be honest, I was initially intimidated. Knowing the importance of first impressions, I had spent a lot of time preparing to ask her just the right question. But when the moment came, all I could think of was "How do you reconcile Catholicism and anarchism?" She looked at me with a bemused expression and said, "It's never been a problem for me."

I withdrew to ponder that, wondering if her words contained some deeper meaning. Over time I came to realize that Dorothy was not greatly interested in abstractions.

She was actually a very social and approachable person. She had little taste for solitude, and it was not hard to get to know her. A great storyteller, she could spin fascinating tales about the Catholic Worker and her comrades in the radical struggle, or poignant details from the life of Chekhov, Tolstoy, or St. Thérèse of Lisieux. She was, in turn, endlessly fascinated by other people's stories—where they came from, what books they liked, where they had traveled. "What's your favorite novel by Dostoyevsky?" was a favorite conversation starter. Whether you answered *The Brothers Karamazov* or *Crime and Punishment,* she inevitably endorsed your selection.

A year after my arrival, Dorothy asked me to become the managing editor of the *Catholic Worker* newspaper. She was, as she liked to say, "in retirement," and the day-to-day management of the paper and the household was in the hands of those she called "the young people." I was twenty. My "promotion" had very little to do with any qualification for the job and everything to do with the fact that no one else was particularly interested. But Dorothy had faith in people, and she was able to make them feel her faith as well, so they forgot their feelings of inadequacy and found themselves doing all kinds of things they never dreamed possible.

She did not much like the rather lugubrious art I selected for my first issue of the paper. "People my age don't want to see dark things like that," she said. "They want to see cheerful things, like the ocean or the circus." Otherwise she exercised little day-to-day oversight. Each month she would give me a few sheets of entries typed up from her journal. "Do what you want with it," she would say. "I don't care if you change it, cut it up, or throw it away." From previous editors I learned that she was not always this detached about her writing. Part of her reason for writing now, she said, was to let her readers know that she was "still alive." Indeed, if she missed a month, we would be besieged by letters inquiring as to her health.

Dorothy admired hard workers. In the "war between the worker and the scholar," she liked people to be both. She did not particularly admire those who were just "scholars," who sat around reading all the time. She thought that men were constitutionally prone to this kind of abstraction, which was responsible for many of the world's problems. (Certainly my own tendencies were in that direction.)

Nevertheless she enjoyed talking about ideas, especially as they were embodied in history, novels, social movements, or people's lives. It was Dorothy who first sparked my fascination with the lives of the saints—both canonized figures like St. Francis of Assisi and St. Teresa of Ávila and other holy people, like Gandhi, Cesar Chavez, and Martin Luther King Jr. She delighted in talking about their human qualities as much as their heroic deeds. "Youth has an instinct for the heroic," she liked to say. And even as she grew bent with age and hard of hearing, she retained her idealism, an instinct for adventure that connected her in a special way with the spirit of youth.

One day I applied under the Freedom of Information Act for a copy of the voluminous FBI file that documented efforts over several decades to comprehend just what category of subversion the Catholic Worker was supposed to represent. Apparently at one time Dorothy's name was placed on a list of dangerous radicals to be detained in the event of a national emergency. What particularly pleased her, however, was a profile that J. Edgar Hoover had composed: "Dorothy Day is a very erratic and irresponsible person who makes every effort to castigate the Bureau whenever she feels inclined."

"That's marvelous!" she said. "Read it again!"

There was a playful side to her. Photographs tend to make her look severe. But what stands out in the memory of anyone who knew Dorothy is her girlish laugh and sense of fun. Many of her stories were self-deprecating—such as the time she knitted a pair of socks, and one of the women in the house asked if she could have them to use as a "gag gift" for Christmas. Or the time in the 1950s when she read a book about Chairman Mao and volunteered to lead a talk at the next Friday night meeting. "Well, somehow word must have spread, because that Friday the room was filled with people from Chinatown and scholars from colleges and universities, and they must have been surprised when all I did was stand up and give a book report. You see," she said, "I'm such a fool that I'm never afraid of appearing foolish."

All the same, she was fastidious and cultivated in her tastes; she loved classical music, the opera, literature, flowers, and beautiful things. In her old age she liked to surround herself with postcards—icons and paintings, but also pictures of nature: trees, the ocean, arctic wilderness. She loved to quote Dostoyevsky's words "The world will be saved by beauty."

Despite all the sadness and suffering around her, she had an eye for the transcendent. There were always moments when it was possible to see beneath the surface. "Just look at that tree!" she would say. An act of kindness, the sound of an opera on the radio, or the sight of flowers growing on the fire escape outside her window—such moments caused her heart to rejoice. She liked to quote St. Teresa of Ávila, who said, "I am such a grateful person that I can be purchased for a sardine."

Above all she was a woman of prayer. She attended daily Mass when she was able; she rose at dawn each day to recite the morning office and to meditate on Scripture. After years of reading the Liturgy of the Hours, the language of the psalms had become her daily bread: "Sing to the Lord a new song. . . . Sing joyfully to the Lord."

When I went to the Catholic Worker, I was not motivated by explicitly religious interests. Like Dorothy, I had been raised in the Episcopal Church, but I had pretty much drifted away from organized religion. What drew me to the Catholic Worker was Dorothy's lifetime of consistent opposition to war, and the fact that her convictions were rooted in solidarity with the poor and those who suffered. Ultimately, I came to appreciate not just Dorothy's antiwar convictions but also the deeper tradition and spirituality that sustained her. I understood nothing about Dorothy if I did not realize the importance of the sacraments, prayer, liturgy, and the communion of saints, in which her witness was rooted. When I understood that, I felt a need to become a Catholic myself.

We were chatting in her room one day when I drew up my courage to say, "There's something I want to talk to you about."

"Yes?"

"Well," I began, "I've been thinking . . . well, thinking is not the right word. Well, I've been . . ." I stumbled along like this for a while, and she just sat there perplexed.

"Well, what is it?" she pressed.

"I'm thinking of becoming a Catholic."

She was very quiet for a few moments, and I wondered whether she had heard me. Finally, she asked, "Well, you're an Episcopalian, right?"

"Yes, that is how I was raised."

"That's what I thought," she said. "My father said only policemen and washerwomen were Catholics and that if I wanted to go to church I could always be an Episcopalian. So I did go to the Episcopal church as I was growing up, and I suppose it did me some good . . . But I always felt the Episcopal Church was a little well-to-do."

She squinted the way she did whenever she was saying something a little mischievous.

I saw her later after I was received into the church in a small chapel in a tenement apartment of the Little Brothers of the Gospel. Dorothy received me with much joy, giving me an old biography of Charles de Foucauld and a cross made out of nails. "No one will dare to arrest you as long as you're wearing that," she said.

She recalled her own first communion, in a church on Staten Island many years before. "I was all flustered with the occasion and I said to a woman, 'Oh, I must get home. I've got a baby to feed.' And the woman said, 'Why, I didn't know you were married.' And I said, 'I'm not.' And you should have seen the expression on her face, wondering whether they hadn't made a terrible mistake!"

It was one of our last conversations. That fall I returned to college to study religion and literature. So many over the years had come and gone at the Catholic Worker. She wished me well and urged me not to forget her. "What is your favorite book by Dostoyevsky?" she asked. "*The Idiot*," I suggested arbitrarily. "Mine too!" she replied with delight.

She died soon after, on November 29, 1980.

That was twenty-five years ago. After her death I would have been delighted to see Dorothy immediately canonized and named the patron saint of peace and social justice. From a distance of twenty-five years, however, I see that she was more than a hero for radical Catholics. At a time when the church is so greatly divided between ideological factions, Dorothy was truly a saint of "common ground"—someone who held in tension a great love for the church along with deep suffering over its sins and failings.

I think about her especially in these times we are living through, when once again the gospel narrative seems somehow foolish and irrelevant in the face of terrorism and endless war. Once again we confront a situation in which massive violence is proffered as the only realistic solution to our problems, and a "just cause" is invoked to justify virtually any means.

I remember sitting with Dorothy over supper while a somewhat deranged young man pounded on the table, insisting: "Dorothy, you just don't understand. Individuals in this day and age are not what's important. It's nations and governments that are important."

"All individuals are important," Dorothy answered, in a quiet voice. "They're all that's important."

But she was equally discerning in her approach to peacemaking, cautioning against the temptation to be overly concerned with "success." Too often, she believed, would-be peacemakers are driven by the need to be heard in the corridors of power, to be impressive and spectacular. But Christ's victory, she always noted, was achieved by way of apparent failure: "Unless the seed falls into the ground and dies, it bears no fruit."

"We do what we can," she often said. Nevertheless, she said, "we must always aim for the impossible; if we lower our goal, we also diminish our effort."

One of her favorite characters was Pietro Spina, the hero of Ignazio Silone's novel *Bread and Wine,* who does no more during a time of war than go out in the night and write the word NO on the town walls. If nothing else, his deed shattered the "unanimity of consent"; it allowed people to envision the subversive possibility of an alternative reality.

Dorothy was a great believer in what Jean-Pierre de Caussade called "the sacrament of the present moment." In each situation, in each encounter, in each task before us, she believed, there is a path to God. We do not need to be in a monastery or a chapel. We do not need to become different people first. We can start today, this moment, where we are, to add to the balance of love in the world, to add to the balance of peace.

It Is Not Power, but Love That Redeems Us!

Pope Benedict XVI

from the homily at his inauguration Mass

At his inauguration, the new pope reflects on the shepherd's mission and the fisherman's task.

Editor's note: Benedict XVI was installed as pope at a Mass in St. Peter's Square on April 24, 2005. In this excerpt from his homily, he explains the meaning of the pallium and the fisherman's ring, the two symbols of his office.

The first symbol is the pallium, woven in pure wool, which will be placed on my shoulders. This ancient sign, which the bishops of Rome have worn since the fourth century, may be considered an image of the yoke of Christ, which the bishop of this city, the servant of the servants of God, takes upon his shoulders. God's yoke is God's will, which we accept. And this will does not weigh down on us, oppressing us and taking away our freedom. To know what God wants, to know where the path of life is found—this was Israel's joy, this was her great privilege. It is also our joy: God's will does not alienate us; it purifies us—even if this can be painful—and so it leads us to ourselves. In this way, we serve not only him, but the salvation of the whole world, of all history.

The symbolism of the pallium is even more concrete: the lamb's wool is meant to represent the lost, sick, or weak sheep that the shepherd places on his shoulders and carries to the waters of life. For the fathers of the church, the parable of the lost sheep, which the shepherd seeks in the desert, was an image of the mystery of Christ and the church. The human race—every one of us—is the sheep lost in the desert that no longer knows the way. The Son of God will not let this happen; he cannot abandon humanity in so wretched a condition. He leaps to his feet and abandons the glory of heaven in order to go in search of the sheep and pursue it, all the way to the cross. He takes it upon his shoulders and carries our humanity; he carries us all—he is the good shepherd who lays down his life for the sheep.

What the pallium indicates first and foremost is that we are all carried by Christ. But at the same time it invites us to carry one another. Hence the pallium becomes a symbol of the shepherd's mission, of which the second reading and the Gospel speak. The pastor must be inspired by Christ's holy zeal: for him it is not a matter of indifference that so many people are living in the desert. And there are so many kinds of desert. There is the desert of poverty, the desert of hunger and thirst, the desert of abandonment, of loneliness, of destroyed love. There is the desert of God's darkness, the emptiness of souls no longer aware of their dignity or the goal of human life. The external deserts in the world are growing, because the internal deserts have become so vast. Therefore the earth's treasures no longer serve to build God's garden for all to live in, but they have been made to serve the powers of exploitation and destruction. The church as a whole and all her pastors, like Christ, must set out to lead people out of the desert, toward the place of life, toward friendship with the Son of God, toward the One who gives us life, and life in abundance.

The symbol of the lamb also has a deeper meaning. In the ancient Near East, it was customary for kings to style themselves shepherds of their people. This was an image of their power, a cynical image: to them their subjects were like sheep, which the shepherd could dispose of as he wished. When the shepherd of all humanity, the living God, himself became a lamb, he stood on the side of the lambs, with those who are downtrodden and killed. This is how he reveals himself to be the true shepherd: "I am the good shepherd. . . . I lay down my life for the sheep," Jesus says of himself (John 10:14–15).

It is not power, but love that redeems us! This is God's sign: he himself is love. How often we wish that God would show himself stronger, that he would strike decisively, defeating evil and creating a better world. All ideologies of power justify themselves in exactly this way; they justify the destruction of whatever would stand in the way of progress and the liberation of humanity. We suffer on account of God's patience. And yet we need his patience. God, who became a lamb, tells us that the world is saved by the crucified One, not by those who crucified him. The world is redeemed by the patience of God. It is destroyed by the impatience of man.

One of the basic characteristics of a shepherd must be to love the people entrusted to him, even as he loves Christ whom he serves. "Feed my sheep," says Christ to Peter, and now, at this moment, he says it to me as well. Feeding means loving, and loving also means being ready to suffer. Loving means giving the sheep what is truly good, the nourishment of God's truth, of God's word; the nourishment of his presence, which he gives us in the Blessed Sacrament. My dear friends—at this moment I can only say: Pray for me, that I may learn to love the Lord more and more. Pray for me, that I may learn to love his flock more and more—in other words, you, the holy church, each one of you and all of you together. Pray for me, that I may not flee for fear of the wolves. Let us pray for one another, that the Lord will carry us and that we will learn to carry one another.

The second symbol used in today's liturgy to express the inauguration of the Petrine ministry is the presentation of the fisherman's ring. Peter's call to be a shepherd, which we heard in the Gospel, comes after the account of a miraculous catch of fish: after a night in which the disciples had let down their nets without success, they see the risen Lord on the shore. He tells them to let down their nets once more, and the nets become so full that they can hardly pull them in—153 large fish, "and although there were so many, the net was not torn" (John 21:11).

This account, coming at the end of Jesus' earthly journey with his disciples, corresponds to an account found at the beginning: there too, the disciples had caught nothing the entire night; there too, Jesus had invited Simon once more to put out into the deep. And Simon, who was not yet called Peter, gave the wonderful reply: "Master, . . . at your word I will let down the nets." And then came the conferral of his mission: "Do not be afraid; henceforth you will be catching men" (Luke 5:1–11).

Today too the church and the successors of the apostles are told to put out into the deep sea of history and to let down the nets, so as to win men and women over to the gospel—to God, to Christ, to true life. The fathers made a very significant commentary on this singular task. This is what they say: For a fish, created for water, it is fatal to be taken out of the sea, to be removed from its vital element to serve as human food. But in the mission of a fisher of men, the reverse is true. We are living in alienation, in the salt waters of suffering and death, in a sea of darkness without light. The net of the gospel pulls us out of the waters of death and brings us into the splendor of God's light, into true life. It is really true: as we follow Christ in this mission to be fishers of men, we must bring men and women out of the sea that is salted with so many forms of alienation and onto the land of life, into the light of God.

It is really so: the purpose of our lives is to reveal God to men. And only where God is seen does life truly begin. Only when we meet the living God in Christ do we know what life is. We are not some casual and meaningless product of evolution. Each of us is the result of a thought of God. Each of us is willed, each of us is loved, each of us is necessary. There is nothing more beautiful than to be surprised by the gospel, by the encounter with Christ. There is nothing more beautiful than to know him and to speak to others of our friendship with him. The task of the shepherd, the task of the fisher of men, can often seem wearisome. But it is beautiful and wonderful, because it is truly a service to joy, to God's joy, which longs to break into the world.

Here I want to add something: both the image of the shepherd and that of the fisherman issue an explicit call to unity. "I have other sheep, that are not of this fold; I must bring them also, and they will heed my voice. So there shall be one flock, one shepherd" (John 10:16); these are the words of Jesus at the end of his discourse on the good shepherd. And the account of the 153 large fish ends with the joyful statement "[A]lthough there were so many, the net was not torn" (John 21:11). Alas, beloved Lord, with sorrow we must now acknowledge that it has been torn! But no—we must not be sad! Let us rejoice because of your promise, which does not disappoint, and let us do all we can to pursue the path toward the unity you have promised. Let us remember it in our prayer to the Lord, as we plead with him: Yes, Lord, remember your promise. Grant that we may be one flock and one shepherd! Do not allow your net to be torn; help us to be servants of unity!

At this point, my mind goes back to October 22, 1978, when Pope John Paul II began his ministry here in St. Peter's Square. His words on that occasion constantly echo in my ears: "Do not be afraid! Open wide the doors for Christ!" The pope was addressing the mighty, the powerful of this world, who feared that Christ might take away something of their power if they were to let him in, if they were to allow the faith to be free. Yes, he would certainly have taken something away from them: the dominion of corruption, the manipulation of law, and the freedom to do as they pleased. But he would not have taken away anything that pertains to human freedom or dignity, or to the building of a just society.

The pope was also speaking to everyone, especially the young. Are we not perhaps all afraid in some way? If we let Christ enter fully into our lives, if we open ourselves totally to him, are we not afraid that he might take something away from us? Are we not perhaps afraid to give up something significant, something unique, something that makes life so beautiful? Do we not then risk ending up diminished and deprived of our freedom? And once again the pope said: No! If we let Christ into our lives, we lose nothing, nothing, absolutely nothing of what makes life free, beautiful, and great. No! Only in this friendship are the doors of life opened wide. Only in this friendship is the great potential of human existence truly revealed. Only in this friendship do we experience beauty and liberation.

And so, today, with great strength and great conviction, on the basis of long personal experience of life, I say to you, dear young people: Do not be afraid of Christ! He takes nothing away, and he gives you everything. When we give ourselves to him, we receive a hundredfold in return. Yes, open, open wide the doors to Christ—and you will find true life. Amen.

Six Recognitions of the Lord

Mary Oliver

from *Shenandoah*

1.
I know a lot of fancy words.
I tear them from my heart and my tongue.
Then I pray.

2.
Lord God, mercy is in your hands, pour
me a little; patience is in your hands,
pour me a little. And tenderness too. My
need is great. Beauty walks so freely
and with such gentleness. Impatience puts
a halter on my face and I run away over
the green fields wanting your voice, your
tenderness, but having to do with only
the sweet grasses of the fields against
my body. When I first found you I was
filled with light, now the darkness grows

and it is filled with crooked things, bitter
and weak, each one bearing my name.

3.
I lounge on the grass, that's all. So
simple. Then I lie back until I am
inside the cloud that is just above me
but very high, and shaped like a fish.
Or, perhaps not. Then I enter the place
of not-thinking, not-remembering, not-
wanting. When the blue jay cries out his
riddle, in his carping voice, I return.
But I go back, the threshold is always
near. Over and back, over and back. Then
I rise. Maybe I rub my face as though I
have been asleep. But I have not been
asleep. I have been, as I say, inside
the cloud, or, perhaps, the lily floating
on the water. Then I go back to town,
to my own house, my own life, which has
now become brighter and simpler, somewhere I have never been before.

4.
Of course I have always known you
are present in the clouds, and the
black oak I especially adore, and the
wings of birds. But you are present
too in the body, listening to the body,
teaching it to live, instead of all
that touching, with disembodied joy.
We do not do this easily. We have

lived so long in the heaven of touch,
and we maintain our mutability, our
physicality, even as we begin to
apprehend to the other world. Slowly we
make our appreciative response.
Slowly appreciation swells to
astonishment. And we enter the dialogue
of our lives that is beyond all understanding or conclusion. It is mystery.
It is love of God. It is obedience.

5.
Oh, feed me this day, Holy Spirit, with
the fragrance of the fields and the
freshness of the oceans which you have
made, and help me to hear and to hold
in all dearness those exacting and wonderful
words of our Lord Christ Jesus, saying:
Follow me.

6.
Every summer the lilies rise
    and open their white hands until they almost
cover the black waters of the pond. And I give
    thanks but it does not seem like adequate thanks,
it doesn't seem
    festive enough or constant enough, nor does the
name of the Lord or the words of thanksgiving come
    into it often enough. Everywhere I go I am
treated like royalty, which I am not. I thirst and
    am given water. My eyes thirst and I am given
the white lilies on the black water. My heart
    sings but the apparatus of singing doesn't convey

half what it feels and means. In spring there's hope,
   in fall the exquisite, necessary diminishing, in
winter I am as sleepy as any beast in its
   leafy cave, but in summer there is
everywhere the luminous sprawl of gifts,
   the hospitality of the Lord and my
inadequate answers as I row my beautiful, temporary body
   through this water-lily world.

Are Young Catholics Embracing Orthodoxy?

Amy Welborn and Others

from Open Book

Catholics have a spirited conversation in cyberspace.

Editor's note: This discussion about young Catholics started on March 3, 2005, on Open Book (http://amywelborn.typepad .com/openbook/), a popular Catholic blog moderated by Amy Welborn. Welborn begins the conversation with a quote from a column in the National Catholic Reporter *by Joe Feuerherd, the paper's Washington correspondent. Welborn then comments on the quote, and a number of comments from her readers follow. The comments have been edited for space. Read the entire discussion at http://amywelborn.typepad.com/openbook/2005/03/a_myth .html#comments.*

Amy Welborn: Joe Feuerherd on some "myths":

> According to some Catholic writers, there is a revitalized "ortho-doxy" among the Catholic young. Papal biographer George Weigel says they are at the forefront of an "authentic Catholic renewal,"

and author Colleen Carroll (*The New Faithful*) writes that "ortho-doxy's appeal seems to be growing among young adults who have a disproportionate amount of cultural influence—those who set trends and lead others in academic, artistic, and political circles."

A case of wishful thinking? At a February 18 presentation on "Commitments and Concerns of Young Adult Catholics," Catholic University of America sociologist Dean Hoge painted a picture of eighteen- to thirty-nine-year-old American Catholics that shat-tered the myth of growing conservatism among this group. Not surprisingly, perhaps, only 22 percent of this age group agreed that it is "always morally wrong" to "engage in premarital sex," though nearly two-thirds of their elders (sixty-three and older) said so. Only 10 percent of younger Catholics agreed that artificial birth control is always wrong. But even outside temptations of the flesh (opportunities for which are presumably greater among the younger population), the overwhelming majority (80 percent) of the gen-eration called to lead this "authentic Catholic renewal" agreed that "individuals should seek out religious truth for themselves and not automatically conform to the doctrines of any church." Eighty-eight percent said, "If you believe in God, it doesn't really matter which religion you belong to." Most didn't even know the Second Vatican Council took place, much less what it taught.

Anyone who's taught in a Catholic high school or religious ed program will greet such findings with a yawn. So? What else is new? One year with my seniors, I asked how many thought premarital sex was wrong. None of them did. Every once in a while, on a Monday, I would poll them on their Mass-attending habits. I'd poll freshmen and seniors both. Most of the (Catholic) freshmen had been to Mass the previous week-end. Maybe 25 percent of the (Catholic) seniors had.

However, what I think is being missed here is Weigel's and Carroll's real point, which is not that Catholic youth as a whole are slouching toward orthodoxy or conservatism, but that that's where the Catholic action is. That's where the energy is. The groups and movements of young Catholics that are growing and active are, for the most part, those that integrate a more holistic vision of Catholicism—by that I mean not one obsessed with "the spirit of Vatican II," but one more interested in the spirit and richness of the entirety of Catholicism, from the Gospels on up to JPII—and are doing that very serious dance of engaging the culture even as they question it and refuse to be co-opted by it. They're involved in the most interesting and energetic apostolates. They're doing the most successful and popular speaking. They're doing the most engaging writing. In ten years, they'll be the ones setting the agenda, I have no doubt.

Todd: It's wishful for adults to think youth are following in their footsteps, but I simply can't see thirtysomething energetics taking Weigel's place in 2015. I suspect the older crowd of neocons will find their positions dear enough to hold on for a good long time. It was that way twenty years ago, and I don't think human nature has changed that much.

R.O.: That even 10 percent of younger Catholics think contraception is always wrong is surprising to me, although I'm a twenty-six-year-old Catholic who thinks it. When I was in a Catholic girls' high school of the Brooklyn Diocese, my impression was that the typical student (at least among the well-behaved, mostly honor-roll types I knew) went to Mass on every day of obligation, planned to remain a virgin until marriage, and utterly disregarded the teaching on contraception. I'm not in touch with enough of them to know what has happened in their lives over the past decade re churchgoing and sex.

Clark: What is certainly the case is that those of my generation (I am twenty-seven) who take their faith seriously (and I am purposely eschewing the labels of orthodoxy and conservatism) will not be taking up the mantle of the

National Catholic Reporter and *U.S. Catholic* and other tired and hackneyed approaches to Catholicism. There is nothing intellectually vibrant about them. And I don't think Weigel thinks these young people are necessarily neocons. He thinks they are young people who have become intoxicated with the gospel of Christ, who are sick and tired of a mansy-pansy Catholicism whose first step is to question so much of tradition. I think he would point to the young folks at Notre Dame who have followed Father Michael Baxter and his radical vision of following Christ as equally as he would to those who have taken a more neocon approach. It isn't a question of one brand of Catholicism or another. It is a question of Catholicism lived in its fullness and richness or half-baked versions that have the attractiveness of a tapeworm.

Donald R. McClarey: I would not draw too many conclusions from loose morality among the very young when it comes to later religious attitudes. One can imagine the type of answers that St. Francis would have given in his playboy days, before his encounter with a talking crucifix. When they are ready, most of the young, especially after parenthood, will follow Mother Church.

Jim: And what is the church in the United States doing to pass on its great treasure of tradition to the next generation? Its parochial school systems are a shambles, and schools are closing at a record rate. Its high schools have become, in effect, private academies with so many nonpracticing (but affluent) students that the faith is presented in a lukewarm, dumbed-down version so as not to really offend anyone. And the majority of students don't go to Catholic schools and are subjected to a religious education program that is "taught" usually by poorly trained and generally uninformed catechists. And the notion of "vocation" is still mostly reserved for vocations to the priesthood and religious life, while we consign the rest of our children to a guidance counseling system that emphasizes how to get the best-paying job, instead of encouraging young people to find a life's work that is compatible with the gifts that God has given them. Some of our young people have figured all of this out and have found the right path on their own, but why are we making it so difficult?

Messy: Where are all these young, devoted Catholics? I'm dying to meet them! They weren't in any of the parishes I attended in Pittsburgh or Baton Rouge or New Orleans or—aside from Notre Dame, a special case—South Bend. I went to the Rite of Election in the Archdiocese of Chicago a few weeks ago and didn't find them there either, though I did see about fifteen hundred Latin Americans. I have seen a lot more curiosity about Catholicism from people my age (I'm twenty-eight), but I've had trouble finding my peer group in an actual PARISH.

B. Knotts: I think there is also a basic cultural/behavioral point to consider: the younger generation tends, to some extent, to rebel against the establishment. The *NCR*/feminist/dissenter crowd is the establishment.

Tom C.: As a twenty-eight-year-old recent convert, I thought I might add a few of my thoughts. First, at seventeen I was an atheist dope-smoking punk rocker. Now I'm a loony ultraconservative Catholic. Go figure. People change a lot between seventeen and twenty-seven, and the trend today is definitely in a more conservative direction. All my old friends, to some degree, have shifted to the right (though not necessarily as much as I have).

Second, I'd have to agree that all the energy and excitement is on the conservative side of the church. When I first became interested in the church and started looking for info on the Internet, everything I found was rather traditional and conservative—Mark Shea, Amy (our host here), Catholic Answers, etc. The folks my age and younger use the Internet for everything, and what they will find is almost all solidly traditional. I did not come across a single liberal Catholic apologetics page. Now, my RCIA class is a different story . . .

I think this parallels a bigger trend in Western civilization. The boomers have pretty much run the show, and their ideological viewpoints mostly solidified in the '60s, when all things old were discarded and all things new were embraced. But the boomers will not be running things for much longer. Those of us who grew up in the '80s and '90s generally don't have such a rosy opinion of personal liberation. We've grown up in a world confronted with the negative consequences of that attitude. We have the option of either embracing that nihilistic reality or rejecting all of it.

For me, the Catholic Church was appealing because it was so rebellious; it was the only institution willing to thumb its nose at the spirit of the age. It was a clear alternative to the banal nihilistic world I had grown up in. And perhaps for that reason I'm more "spirit of Trent" than "spirit of Vatican II."

AnotherCoward: My real name is Spencer. I consider myself an orthodox Catholic (this is where you all clap for me and give me hugs and stuff). I'll be twenty-seven soon. I'm a convert of four years this Easter. I'm married to a wife who is without a doubt best suited for me. I'm a father of two boys. Up until we had the kids, we were super involved with the teens at our parish—now, with babies and toddlers, not so much. And there are others like me. Not a lot, but they are there. And we *LOVE* our faith, just as someone said: all of it, from Adam to the Gospels through today and on into tomorrow.

The biggest problem I think for us is our small number. That's something perhaps that we're left to fix. But, as with any kind of real evangelization, it is hard. It's hard for me to talk with people my own age at my own parish or in casual settings because of their blatant disregard for the teachings of our faith. It's really hard to evangelize as a Catholic because you're not simply presenting the gospel to someone—you're presenting church history and redefining it for people who have only heard about the Spanish Inquisition and the Crusades and the Reformation. You've got to get Protestants out of *sola scriptura*: something that is increasingly possible as they begin to study and emphasize biblical historical context (which is why I was won over). And you've got to get people back to the concept of church: the marriage of autonomy and community. But it's not until you really enter the church, sacrificing autonomy—which we are taught is king and absolute to who we are—for an equitable relationship between autonomy and community, that you become orthodox (in my humble opinion). So, yeah, we're here . . . yeah, there's not a whole lot of us . . . but we do exist.

John Sheridan: At thirty-five I am certainly not young, but I am younger than the *NCR* generation. And the one thing I think may be unique about the *NCR* types is that they manage to be very devoted to Catholicism without believing in anything that Catholicism actually teaches. I don't think this trait will continue down the generations; I suspect that it was the result of some sort of cultural connection with Catholicism that no longer exists. I think people of my generation and younger tend to make a choice. If they like women priests, gay marriage, etc., then they will leave the church—I mean, what is the point of staying? They can become Episcopalian.

Mike Roesch: In my experience, this generation is all or nothing, orthodox or apathetic. There are very, very few "progressive" Catholics in my generation; the youth who disagree with the church (and there are a lot of them) just leave. This contrasts with the previous generations who stuck around to try to change things. The ones who do stay in the church don't come to Mass, and they certainly don't become priests. There will be no Father [Richard] McBriens in this generation.

Daniel H. Conway: Ignored by the conservative crowd is the army of faith-based postgraduate volunteers and Catholic Workers. Jesuit Volunteers, Mercy Corps, Maryknoll are easy examples. Almost all these folks are young. What is it about this example of sacrifice, if only temporary, that it can be routinely ignored by Weigel, et al.? What isn't said in conservative circles is as predictable as what is said.

Sean Gallagher: I remember working as a director of religious education and hearing the assumption from the pastor that young adults who were nominal Catholics would become more active when they started having children and wanting to have them baptized, etc. I believe that that may have been true at one time. It's not now. It is quite socially acceptable to openly and directly reject the practice of any faith in particular or all in general. Indeed, I think society is moving in the direction where it will be less and less acceptable to actually embrace the practice of a traditional Christian faith with a high degree of enthusiasm.

Mark: The future of young Catholics, I believe, doesn't (and should not) lie in one direction. And while it's encouraging to see the witness of young Catholics excited about the faith like the students of the Compass organization I work with here at Loyola University New Orleans, I am concerned for the many young Catholics who, for various reasons, are alienated from the church. They are a diverse bunch and aren't necessarily going to fall in line with traditions within Catholicism that you or I might prefer, but I'm convinced nevertheless there is a place for them. And I'm not satisfied, like some seem to be, with just giving up on them because they don't fit our mold. What are we going to do to invite them back into the Body of Christ?

Sister Rosemarie Wants You

Clare Ansberry

from *The Wall Street Journal*

The Little Sisters of the Poor have an odd business plan for nursing homes: beg for help, lavish it on residents.

With the cost and quality of care for the elderly looming as increasingly urgent problems, the Little Sisters of the Poor in Pittsburgh have an unusual solution: they beg.

One recent day, two nuns in white habits stood quietly in a dimly lit produce warehouse. Around them, workers wheeled carts stacked high with sacks of potatoes. Outside, trucks rumbled up to the concrete loading docks with their 8:00 a.m. deliveries.

When the owner of the warehouse hung up the phone, Sister Rosemarie stepped forward with a request vital to the dwindling order's mission: did he have any vegetables to spare? The owner nodded to one of his workers to get a fifty-pound bag of carrots and two boxes of eggplants. The second nun, Sister Marcella, her back and shoulders curved from arthritis and degenerating disks, lifted her head and thanked the man.

The two nuns wound their way around boxes of sweet-smelling Georgia peaches, reviewing in low whispers what they would ask of the next distributor on their weekly rounds at the Strip, this city's open-air produce market. A thin man with a cigarette gave them a case of broccoli and chopped romaine. A coffee roaster provided five pounds of dark roast and a pound of chocolate-raspberry blend.

At the huge Consumers Produce warehouse, Joe McCain scoffed at Sister Marcella's request for a watermelon. "One watermelon?" he asked skeptically. Without waiting for her response, he said he was giving her four.

The nuns brought a vanload of donated food back to their block-long brick home. There, they and eight other Little Sisters of the Poor care for sixty elderly residents, age seventy to one hundred. Begging to provide for the impoverished elderly defines their order and has sustained it for more than a century.

As the baby boomers age and anxiety grows about elder care, the Little Sisters and their begging tradition are an anomaly. They provide poor residents with high-quality care—individual rooms and lots of individual attention—on a tight budget. Almost 90 percent of the residents here have assets of less than ten thousand dollars. More than half have none at all. Residents pay if and what they can. Typically, the sisters accept only a third of a person's income from pension or Social Security.

While nursing homes—even those catering to the poor—generally rely on government programs, private insurance, and fees paid by residents for most of their income, the Little Sisters follow a more difficult path. They receive no continuing help from the Vatican or the local diocese. If offered an endowment, they would refuse. Instead, the nuns beg for food, for clothes, for money, and for special wheelchairs. Donations account for about 60 percent of their annual five-million-dollar budget. The rest comes from Medicaid, Medicare, Social Security, and other sources.

Their model isn't easily replicated, nor is it necessarily desirable. They face a declining population of nuns. Begging for contributions to renovate or expand can take a long time—or not work at all. Homes in Detroit and New Orleans closed, as did a second home in Pittsburgh. Begging gets harder when the economy tanks or when disasters, like Katrina, divert donations elsewhere. Costs of food, medicine, and energy are rising.

Yet the sisters here have plans to expand, converting an old wing into apartments for dozens more elderly poor. Instead of looking for a long-term source of funds, such as an endowment, they rely on divine providence and the attentive ear of their patron, St. Joseph. "It's not the way of the world," says Sister Mary Vincent. "People think it's stupid. I talk to them, and I know they're thinking, *My God, these people are in outer space.*"

An advisory board staffed by local CEOs and bankers gives the nuns financial advice, such as how to save money on nutritional supplements and cleaning materials as well as contracts with elevator maintenance companies. But the nuns refuse to budge when it comes to suggestions that they cut corners on construction or offer fewer amenities.

James Will, chairman of the advisory board and former CEO of Armco Steel, recalls a nun asking him: "Would you like to go to heaven and stand before St. Peter and say, 'I lived in a wonderful and beautiful home, but when it came to putting together a home for the poor, I gave them a cheaper version'?"

"They're unshakable in their belief that they're doing God's will, and because they're willing to do it, they will never be let down," says Mr. Will. "It's hard for us in the everyday world, fighting financial battles, to understand."

Unlike at many nursing homes, every resident at the Little Sisters' home has a private room. Those who can't dress themselves are dressed each day in their favorite outfits, including jewelry. Men are clean shaven. The sisters throw festive Mardi Gras parties with shrimp étouffée. White wine is offered with Sunday dinners.

The nuns work hard to make sure no one dies alone. One nun sits by the bedside of the gravely ill throughout the day. When she feels death is near, she alerts the others by beeper, summoning them from meetings, Mass, and errands to the room, where they pray and sing.

There is little staff turnover among the lay workers here. The average length of service is twelve and a half years. By contrast, between a third and a fourth of the nation's long-term-care workers have less than a year's experience. Residents here live an average of six to seven years, compared with the nationwide average for nursing homes of two to three years.

"If I had my own home, I wouldn't be any happier," says Cecilia Hugo, who has lived with the sisters for seventeen years.

The order was founded in 1839 by Jeanne Jugan, who came across a destitute elderly blind woman in the streets of a small town in France. She carried the woman back to her apartment and placed the woman in her own bed. To feed the woman and others who followed, Jeanne Jugan went house to house, begging for food.

The order maintains a global reach, with 206 nursing homes scattered from Bangalore to Paris, serving about fifteen thousand people. But as fewer women choose to join religious orders, their mission is becoming harder. A century ago, there were fifty-four hundred Little Sisters worldwide. Now there are three thousand. No one has joined the Little Sisters in Pittsburgh for about eight years.

Sister Rosemarie, a short, energetic woman with a deep laugh, is the designated begging nun. In her early fifties, she is one of the younger nuns here. She was born in the Philippines, immigrated to Montreal, obtained a fine-arts degree in interior design, and worked in a department store. Though she was baptized Catholic, her family wasn't particularly religious. After college, she began going to church, met the Little Sisters, and joined the convent.

New in her begging position, she admits mixed feelings. She misses being with the residents. "I'm out of the house so much I feel out of the loop," she says. Demands are relentless, with food obtained one week needing to be replenished the next.

Sister Rosemarie goes about it methodically. Monday is reserved for getting produce and twenty loaves of fresh bread from a bakery. Tuesday she visits local grocery stores, hunting for donations of meat that is still good enough to eat but has passed its sell-by date. Another day is devoted to Costco for leftover pastries and muffins. Thursday she heads to the Pittsburgh food bank.

Between visits to two wholesalers on a recent day, she dialed a third on her cell phone to see if it would give her popcorn for an upcoming carnival. That call complete, she made another to a paint store to see if it would donate a few gallons to paint the basement.

Wherever Sister Rosemarie goes, she takes her place in line. Someone once told her she shouldn't have to. "Yes, I do. That's what the poor have to do. You wait in line," she says.

Sister Mary Vincent must keep her focus on longer-term concerns. Earlier this year, the Little Sisters completed a sixteen-million-dollar addition and chapel renovation, raising the entire amount over five years through donations from individuals and foundations. Now the sisters are embarking on a second, eight-million-dollar phase to convert an old wing into independent-living apartments to house an additional forty-nine residents. Though the construction project would likely qualify for federal low-income housing grants, the sisters won't use them because they don't want the government dictating whether they can add a sitting room or more closet space. That leaves asking people for money, a long and tedious process and one that she doesn't especially like.

"Fund-raising is a pain," she says. Filled with uncertainty, the process leaves the sisters' projects beholden to the fortunes of others, as well as the local economy. She concedes it would be easier to look for long-term funding, but the tradition passed down by their founder requires that they live hand to mouth. They only seek enough money to address their current needs, whether that means lunch tomorrow or a new wing.

"I pray to God asking why it has to be this way, but I know why he's doing it this way," Sister Mary Vincent says. "He wants more people involved in the work of helping the poor."

Lately, she has been sending the nuns out more often into the community to raise both money and public awareness of their mission. Traveling in pairs, they knocked on doors of new homes in high-income developments, looking for contributions. They went to the Pittsburgh International Airport, setting up metal folding chairs and a table near the entrance, across the hall from the Salvation Army representatives and their red kettle. Rushed travelers stared straight ahead, avoiding eye contact with the nuns. Others stopped, often asking the sisters to pray for a family member or friend.

Begging makes Sister Mary Vincent, who tends to hang back behind the other sisters, uncomfortable. "All these people coming at you, wondering who you are and what you're doing. People challenge you. 'How come you're out here begging? You get Medicaid.' Or 'I heard you got five thousand dollars in the last collection. Why are you back out here?'" she says. Trying to ignore their comments, she tells herself that she isn't begging for herself but for the poor. "That doesn't take the sting out of begging if you have any pride," she says. "People think you're doing it for yourself."

Teams of sisters are dispatched on weekends to area churches. On a recent Sunday morning, near the end of the 7:30 Mass at Church of the Resurrection, Sister Marcella and Sister Katherine Ann received Holy Communion and then walked briskly toward the back of the church. Each picked up a green-felt-lined wicker basket that held a single piece of paper with the words *Little Sisters of the Poor.* They stationed themselves on either side of the back doors.

As Mass ended, the church emptied. The sisters stood quietly. People filed by, dipping their hands in a font of holy water, making the sign of the cross, and dropping dollar bills into the basket. Many had already contributed during the regular church collection and simply nodded at the sisters.

The sisters used to bring in a fair share of donations by stationing themselves outside factory gates. But in a less industrial, more secular age, they rely more on special fund-raisers.

On a recent afternoon, the nuns and some residents gathered at a parking lot filled with 250 motorcycles. Sister Mary Vincent was pleased. The weather was good, the crowd big and festive. Beefy motorcyclists wearing bandannas and tattoos, their shoulder-length hair in ponytails, bought raffle tickets for a 165-piece tool kit and a hypnotherapy session.

Eighty-nine-year-old Anna DiRenna, who has lived with the Little Sisters for seventeen years, buzzed in her electric wheelchair between the rows of motorcycles with license plates like VROOM and BECHA.

Sister Mary Vincent thanked John Cigna, a big man with an unlit cigar in his mouth. A local newscaster and biker, Mr. Cigna organized the event. He lined up members of HOG, which stands for Harley Owners Group, and the American Legion Riders. Each biker paid twenty-five dollars to ride the sixty-mile course and return for a cookout and music by Jimmy Sapienza's Five Guys Named Moe. Mr. Cigna remembered the Little Sisters visiting his mother when he was a young boy.

Father Jerome Dixon, former chaplain for the house and now a resident, stood up on a chair. The crowd hushed. Heads bowed. "We ask your blessings on these vehicles, which carry out friends on the journey this day. Keep them from all harm," he said.

After, the riders roared out of the parking lot. A dozen residents, mostly women wearing plastic visors and dark sunglasses, lined the curb, waving with one hand, purse in the other. The event raised five thousand dollars.

The following day, two nuns sat outside a Giant Eagle supermarket in metal folding chairs. They sold raffle tickets for a grandfather clock and cookbooks filled with recipes from the nuns and their residents, raising a few hundred dollars.

Sister Mary Vincent recalls a banker-adviser telling her that he sometimes couldn't sleep at night worrying about how the Little Sisters would finance needed renovations with such piecemeal donations. She told him to have faith. "I really can say I've never lost a night's sleep," she says.

In Praise of Horizontal Prayer

Frank Moan, SJ

from *America*

A retired priest reflects on supine prayer.

I'm seventy-seven and retired, a priest, a celibate. You may be like me. Or you may be married still, with or without your spouse. You may be a parent, a grandparent, or, God bless you, a great-grandparent. Or you may be single, young, with the expectation of many years ahead. In any event, I hope each of you shares with me the joy of horizontal prayer. By horizontal prayer I mean, literally, horizontal: when I'm on my back, in bed. Age has taught me that I do some of my best praying in bed. I still advocate that parents teach their children to kneel at bedside in the evening to say their prayers. But my knees will no longer let me get down there. And if I did get down, I would have to call out to someone else in the rectory to get me up. God understands. In fact, I think God can't wait till I get flat on my back in bed.

I do my best praying then. Sometimes, if I've had a very long and stressful day, I might fall asleep almost immediately.

But that is rare. Generally, I have to lie there for a while before sleep comes. That's when I pray.

I converse with God about the day I've spent, how it went, where I failed God or my neighbor, what graces came my way, and how well I used them. I like to talk to God about the people I encountered that day, in person, on the phone, through e-mail or snail mail. I often tell God how I disagree with the way he is letting the world turn round. I pray for those who die each day in Iraq or Afghanistan. I pray for understanding among Muslims, Christians, and Jews.

I also turn often to Mary, the mother of Jesus. I say at least one Hail Mary to win our Lady's protection. My life in the liturgical practices of the church has taught me that the day never ends without recourse to our Lady.

Prayer to Mary then turns my mind to the communion of saints. Over the years I have come to love and respect so many of them that I count them intimate friends on whom I can depend to be voices for me before the Trinity. And in that number I include many people I have known over these past seventy-seven years who have preceded me to the pearly gates.

At my age—and those who are about my age will know what I'm talking about—I have to get up periodically to relieve my bladder. I take a nightly pill to forestall such an occurrence. But it never does. I think I take the pill just to keep my doctor happy. Anyway, I get up at least twice a night and return to bed. Now sometimes I am lucky and soon fall back to sleep. But often it is not so easy.

So here I am again, turning to prayer. I begin to think about the next day. And the first thing I think is: *Will I have a next day? Or will God summon me before then?* It is not a pessimistic thought. Many of my relatives and friends have died before this age. The daily obituary notices recount many deaths of people my age, older, and younger. So I'm wont to say that prayer I learned in childhood. It may be childish, but it is a beautiful prayer and means a great deal to me at this age: "Now I lay me down to sleep; I pray the Lord my soul to keep. If I should die before I wake, I pray the Lord my soul to take." Some of my fellow Jesuits have died peacefully in their sleep or while sitting in their chair. I envy them—it's a nice way to go.

Then I turn to the coming day, if God should grant it. I recall the intention for the Mass I will celebrate. It may be for a deceased brother Jesuit, or for a relative with cancer, or for our country in this time of national crisis. I talk to God about that intention. I bring God up to date on where I am politically, charitably, socially. I must admit I do much of the talking. But sometimes God does get through. I begin to see things more clearly. I realize there were times I was hasty in judgment or insensitive in action. I see new ideas opening up before me on how I can contribute to the graces God spreads through his church, particularly through its sacramental life.

I give some thought also to the Divine Office, the breviary, I shall be reading when I get up. It will take some time over the course of the day. Nowadays I pray it with much more devotion than I did in my earlier years. I give extra attention to it because I now read it on behalf of all the priests in my diocese. I know many of them are too busy to read it, so I read it for them.

The middle of the night gives me the time to raise to God the many friends I have from over seventy years, particularly those who are now in physical distress. A ninety-two-year-old friend prays daily that she may die. I ask, God, why don't you let her die? She would be so much happier with you than she is now with a body that refuses to respond to her willingness to love others. I pray for my friend the doctor who, shortly after retiring, suffered a debilitating stroke. Since then he has lost a leg and, worse still, much of his enthusiasm for life. I pray for his wife, a nurse with physical problems of her own that prevent her from giving her husband the full attention he needs.

Dear God, you know what wonderful people these have been, how much they have done for others in very active lives. Yet now they wait. God, give them patience; give them cheer. I pray for a widow friend of forty years' acquaintance. Not only has she lost her husband; she also buried two of her five children. Yes, she has the others to look after her. But God, she is failing. Give her courage; give her comfort. And give her children the willingness to look after her, without depriving their own children of the attention they deserve.

I could stay up all night praying for these and myriad other causes.

On a rare occasion nowadays I am awakened by the alarm to rise and go to a nearby parish to say early Mass. That breaks my momentum of prayer.

Ordinarily I can get up when I wake up. Or I can lie there for a few or many minutes. I can pray again. Today, dear God, this day is for you. You have given me another day to live, or maybe only part of the day. If you call me home today, I hope I shall be rejoicing to greet you. But if I am to live another day, may it be to your glory. Let me bring sunshine into someone else's life; let me be a support to my fellow Jesuits here in the rectory; let me learn how to converse with you, dear God, more and more. Teach me to pray.

I open my eyes. I look to see if the sun is shining on the church school building outside my window. How I am cheered if it is. I see in my room all the souvenirs of a long life. They speak to me of so many past and present loves. They are my daily comforts. Each speaks a prayer to me; I speak a prayer to each.

Then it is time to rise. As I put my feet into my slippers, I offer a final prayer. God, I'm going about the day. I may not be as attentive to you throughout this day as I have been during this night. So please remember that I love you still. I'm here to do your will. And should you bring me to another night, I'll lie again in bed, and our conversation will go on.

The Redemption of
Shane Paul O'Doherty

Kevin Cullen

from *The Boston Globe*

He was an IRA terrorist who once tried to kill a bishop. Now he's studying to be a priest.

"Let's go for a walk," Shane Paul O'Doherty says. The Long Corridor at St. Patrick's College, Ireland's last remaining seminary, is a vision out of Harry Potter's school, Hogwarts, dark and slightly foreboding. The oak walls are lined with solemn portraits of clerics who have educated more than eleven thousand Roman Catholic priests since 1795. Inside College Chapel, heels click on the marble mosaic floor, under the gaze of a procession of saints and angels painted on the ceiling. Outside, the three Gothic buildings that form St. Mary's Square overlook a lush garden and a pond with rocks positioned as stepping-stones, designed to symbolize man's spiritual journey toward God.

In the sleepy college town of Maynooth, fifteen miles outside Dublin, we walk through a stone archway into an idyllic Gothic quadrangle called St. Joseph's Square, gravel paths snaking through grassy swaths dappled with bright red flowers. The only sound is birdsong. At fifty, O'Doherty still boasts a boyish appearance: thin and fit, bone-china skin, brown hair closely cropped.

Between 1993 and 2002, seven seminaries closed in Ireland, leaving only St. Patrick's. Though it reeks of history, it also seems a lonely place. In the 1960s, as many as six hundred seminarians studied at St. Patrick's; today, sixty do, a drop that's been attributed both to a more materialistic Ireland and to the country's own ongoing clergy sex abuse scandals, which mirror those in Boston and other American dioceses.

The last time O'Doherty and I went for a long walk together, a decade ago, I was covering the conflict in Northern Ireland for the *Globe,* and he was a married man six years removed from prison. Before his arrest, he'd become the most wanted man in Britain, a hero for the Irish Republican Army whose letter-bomb campaign had maimed a dozen people and terrorized all of London. We walked the streets of Derry, his hometown. At that time, we paused at the rooming house for British soldiers where he had planted his first bomb in 1970, when he was fifteen. We passed the spot in the Bogside where Barney McGuigan's brains had spilled out onto the pavement on Bloody Sunday, in 1972, when British paratroopers shot and killed fourteen civil rights demonstrators. We walked by the apartment in Crawford Square that O'Doherty used as a bomb factory, the one that blew up, killing Ethel Lynch, his twenty-two-year-old assistant.

He was given his middle name because he was born on the Feast of the Conversion of St. Paul, who was a zealous killer of Christians before his own conversion on the road to Damascus. But O'Doherty's story is not about a miraculous religious conversion as much as a gradual spiritual evolution. He had a tug-of-war with God, and God won. His odyssey, from teenage revolutionary to middle-aged seminarian, is a story of redemption.

"Hell," he says, shrugging. "If I can be saved, anyone can."

In 1965, when he was ten years old, he tore a sheet of paper from a book he used to copy lessons in at school and wrote down a pledge: "When I grow up, I, Shane Paul O'Doherty, want to fight and, if necessary, die for Ireland's freedom." Even at his tender age, he knew his words were treasonous, and so he hid them under the floorboards of the attic of his family's home and forgot about them until ten years later, when he was sitting in an interrogation room, under arrest, and a detective shoved the yellowed paper under his nose. He blushed, more embarrassed by his childish idealism than terrified at the prospect of spending the rest of his life in prison.

O'Doherty was born in Derry in 1955 during a winter so cold his mother called him the Snow Baby. Unlike most of Northern Ireland, Derry had a Catholic majority and an established Catholic middle class, one of the reasons the Catholic civil rights movement bloomed there in the late 1960s. O'Doherty was part of that middle class, one of eight children in a family that wasn't especially political. His father was a teacher and principal at a school run by the Christian Brothers, a Catholic order. His mother hailed from a prominent business family. Two of his uncles fought the British in Ireland's war of independence in the 1920s. But O'Doherty's father never spoke of any of this and quietly aspired to unity with the Irish Republic while opposing violence as a means of achieving it. Despite holding the majority in Derry, Catholics were excluded from power through gerrymandering and other discriminatory practices of the Protestant unionist government that was loyal to Britain.

Most of O'Doherty's neighbors were Protestant, and he never heard a sectarian word in his home. But as a child, he would sit alone in his family's well-stocked library, reading about Irish history. "There was something about the tragedy of British rule in Ireland against the wishes of the Irish people," he says.

He was spellbound reading about the Easter Rising of 1916, when a quixotic band of patriots staged a rebellion they knew was doomed, determined to ignite a wider revolution. As a ten-year-old living in British-controlled Northern Ireland, Shane O'Doherty offered himself up to martyrdom, which was something of an empty pledge, not because of his age but because, at the time, there was no rebellion to join. The IRA, widely regarded as a small bunch of dreamers, was dormant.

But that all changed when the Protestant government's response to the demands of the Catholic civil rights movement was to beat protesters off the streets. In 1968 and 1969, around the time O'Doherty was turning fourteen, Derry convulsed with protest and attacks on demonstrators by loyalist mobs and the predominantly Protestant police force. By the time British troops were deployed, O'Doherty had thrown Molotov cocktails at police, and the IRA had become active again. A new group, the Provisional IRA, or the Provos, had sprung up, determined to bring the fight to the British, and fifteen-year-old Shane O'Doherty began an almost farcical search for them, knocking on doors, so he could join. He eventually found two men who inducted him into the secret organization.

"I was no longer an insignificant teenager," he says now. "I became heroic overnight. I felt almost drunk with power."

At sixteen, he threw nail bombs at British soldiers and almost hoped he'd be shot dead, fantasizing that his sacrifice would inspire a mural or, better yet, a song, ensuring his immortality. He jumped out of alleys firing a revolver at soldiers armed with automatic rifles. In 1971, he loosed a rocket at a British army observation tower. It missed but hit another army post by dumb luck. Soldiers then opened fire on a passing car, wounding a woman and two children. O'Doherty went home and prayed that the woman and children would survive. They did, but his having almost caused their deaths had shaken him. He stopped reporting for duty.

Any chance he would stay away from the IRA for good evaporated five days after his seventeenth birthday, however, when British paratroopers opened fire on Catholic demonstrators on January 30, 1972—what became known as Bloody Sunday. He saw unarmed men and teens gunned down. In the chaos, he bumped into a priest he knew, and the two went to the local morgue, where O'Doherty saw police and soldiers laugh and joke about the shootings. He accompanied the priest to the homes of the dead and the injured, and his fury smoldered. He reported back to the IRA and was flattered when his commander eventually asked him to go to London to launch a letter-bomb campaign.

"I had come to the conclusion that all these British soldiers from working-class backgrounds that we were shooting and blowing up in Northern Ireland were deemed expendable by the British government," he says. "The idea was to have those in high places in British military and political circles face the consequences of occupying Ireland."

Once in London, he posed as a student and bought a copy of *Who's Who,* to draw up a target list. One of his bombs injured Reginald Maudling, the British cabinet member in charge of security on Bloody Sunday. He sent a bomb to Bishop Gerard Tickle, the Roman Catholic chaplain to the British army, after reading a newspaper story quoting Tickle as saying British soldiers did nothing wrong on Bloody Sunday. (Tickle later called the story a "press misrepresentation.") The bomb, stuffed into a hollowed-out Bible, failed to detonate. He sent a letter bomb to 10 Downing Street, the prime minister's residence, and it sat unnoticed in a wastebasket for twenty-four hours. It didn't explode, but O'Doherty's ability to pierce security at the heart of the government made him, as the mystery letter-bomber, the most wanted man in Britain.

Other bombs he sent exploded at the London Stock Exchange, the Bank of England, and a government building. The injured included secretaries and security guards, and, as a result, O'Doherty's doubts returned. He went back to Derry to fight on the home front and knelt in a confessional at St. Eugene's Cathedral, where he had been a choirboy a few years and a whole lifetime before. He told the priest he was in the IRA and wanted to talk about the morality of violence in a liberation struggle. But the priest was in no mood to debate.

"Murder and violence are always wrong," the cleric told him.

O'Doherty left that church a more tormented nineteen-year-old than when he entered. But he continued fighting.

In 1975, the IRA called a cease-fire, with the promise from authorities that IRA operatives would not be arrested as a political compromise was hashed out. But that promise turned out to be empty, and in May 1975, police descended on the house of O'Doherty's mother. Sarah O'Doherty, who had no idea her son was in the IRA, was making him lunch; she looked on in bewilderment as he was bundled into a car, shirtless, and whisked away.

The IRA shot a police officer in retaliation for O'Doherty's arrest. The dead cop was the son of the chief officer at the Belfast prison where O'Doherty was being held, and the guards beat the twenty-year-old mercilessly the next day. Guards ripped sheets into long strips and placed them in his cell, advising him to hang himself, because it would be better than what they had planned for him. One guard sat outside his cell and turned the light on and off so O'Doherty couldn't sleep. Years later, the warden who had presided over his torture was murdered by the IRA, and O'Doherty could not muster sympathy for him.

In September, O'Doherty was flown to London and charged with the letter bombings. As he prepared for his trial, he read the reports that chronicled in clinical and shocking detail the extent of the injuries he had inflicted on twelve people. A secretary was blinded by glass in her eyes. A security guard had his hand blown off and an eye blown out. Another man lost the tips of his fingers.

Even as O'Doherty second-guessed himself, he remained defiant. He refused to recognize the authority of the court that tried him in London. The feeling was somewhat mutual, as the elderly judge frequently nodded off. But the judge woke up long enough to give O'Doherty thirty life sentences.

If St. Paul's transformation was on the road to Damascus, O'Doherty's was in solitary confinement in Wormwood Scrubs, a London prison. His conversion was in the monastic tradition of Ireland. For more than a year, he was isolated in a cell, where he read books on the theory of a just war.

"I was trying to justify the violence I had used," he says.

Where guards saw only a stubborn man who refused to wear prison clothing and who insisted he was a political prisoner, the Reverend Gerald Ennis, the Catholic chaplain, saw a pilgrim.

"Your little brother is an extraordinary young man given very special gifts, and I believe those gifts are going to be used for the greater glory of God," Ennis wrote in a prescient letter to one of O'Doherty's brothers in 1977. "I have never worried particularly about his being in the [solitary] block, because he was always a person who was searching for the truth. Once the discovery was made, his prison cell became a monastic cell where he was alone with God and his own thoughts."

O'Doherty emerged from solitary still defiant toward a prison regime he saw as needlessly cruel, but he was changed. At great personal risk, he left the security of the IRA, associating with English prisoners at a time when the Irish in England were held collectively responsible for ongoing IRA violence.

Back in his cell, he began reading the Bible more intently. The Gospel of St. Matthew nagged at him, especially one passage:

> So when you are offering your gift at the altar, if you remember that your brother or sister has something against you, leave your gift there before the altar and go; first be reconciled to your brother or sister, and then come and offer your gift.

"I had rejected the church's doctrine of a just war," O'Doherty says. "I had come to believe that only pacifism was truly moral, truly Christlike. But as I was trying to make myself a better person, to distance myself from the violence I had committed, I couldn't really move forward until I had addressed my victims."

O'Doherty then did what no other IRA member ever had: he apologized to his victims. He never heard back from them, though one, the security guard who had lost an eye and a hand, told British newspapers he opposed the prospect of O'Doherty being released from prison. O'Doherty said he didn't expect or need to be forgiven. The point was his being able to apologize and admit he was wrong.

In September 1985, after demanding repatriation for a decade, O'Doherty got into a taxi with two guards for the drive to Birmingham's airport and a short flight to Belfast. One of the guards handed him a religious paperback. Inside was an inscription from the guard saying that he and his wife had been praying for O'Doherty for months. After ten years of abuse, physical and psychological, in British jails, O'Doherty left the country with tears in his eyes, moved by an Englishman's kindness.

Upon his release in 1989, O'Doherty enrolled at Trinity College in Dublin, pursuing a degree in English and writing his autobiography. A few years later, he met a pretty blonde from Chicago named Michelle Sweeney, who was getting a doctorate in medieval history. They married, settling into a small house in Dublin. He got a job as a computer software trainer. As he prospered in Ireland's booming high-tech economy, he tried to soothe a troubled conscience. He edited a magazine sold by the homeless. He volunteered to help Bosnian Muslim refugees. He taught computer skills to children from itinerant families.

Sweeney accepted an offer to teach in the United States, but O'Doherty could not get a visa to live there because of his criminal record. In the late 1990s, even as other former IRA members who never expressed remorse for their violent deeds flitted in and out of the United States promoting the peace process, O'Doherty was repeatedly denied permission to enter.

O'Doherty and Sweeney's separation caused the marriage to collapse. Sweeney sent him an e-mail saying she wanted a divorce. O'Doherty wanted an annulment. He wrote a fifty-page letter to the board that oversees annulments in the Archdiocese of Chicago. He got his wish.

In the spring of 2001, O'Doherty was sitting at his desk in Stockholm, where he had begun working for Ericsson, the mobile-phone maker. He was a former terrorist, former prisoner, former husband. He had a good salary, and he was miserable. He decided to go back to Dublin. In just a generation, Ireland had gone from being one of Europe's poorest countries to one of its richest. But the sudden, widespread materialism disturbed O'Doherty.

The priesthood intrigued him; it had even when he was a kid. But if his record precluded his getting into the United States, how could he possibly get into a seminary?

On a religious retreat, a priest sidled up to him and asked him if he had ever been on a retreat before.

"Yes," O'Doherty said.

"How long was it?" the priest asked.

"Fourteen and a half years," O'Doherty replied.

In the basement kitchen of Dublin's procathedral, on the city's gritty Northside, Gemma and Triona King, spinster sisters in their fifties, are making sandwiches and explaining how they became two of the approximately two dozen consecrated virgins in Ireland. Their virginity is a gift to God, a symbolic gesture of their giving themselves to serve Jesus Christ. They have worked with Dublin's disadvantaged for years. They also offer intercessions, or prayers, for those who want to become priests. They realized something was up when O'Doherty, who had been volunteering around the cathedral and visiting inmates with the prison chaplain, asked them to pray for him.

"We encouraged Shane," Gemma King says, sipping tea as O'Doherty and another seminarian stand in another part of the kitchen making plans to visit a homeless shelter. "Shane has sinned, like all of us. But he knows the power of repentance, of forgiveness, of redemption, of God's love, not as abstract concepts but as real life. What better qualities could you have for a priest?"

Walking the grounds at the seminary, O'Doherty acknowledges he could do good works as a layperson. But becoming a priest, with five to seven years of intense study and soul-searching, was to him the logical, spiritual conclusion of his odyssey, something he calls "my journey through the largely unknown, praying for the three gifts I have never had: humility, patience, and gentleness."

However long it takes him to be ordained, at fifty he is still ten years younger than the average priest in Dublin.

Gone are the days of long, flowing black cassocks. In jeans and sweaters, the seminarians blend in with the five thousand other students who, since 1997, have shared the bucolic campus that is National University of Ireland, Maynooth.

O'Doherty was elected class representative by his twenty-seven classmates, the largest seminary class in Ireland in more than twenty years.

"What's the difference between a terrorist and a liturgist?" a priest asked the seminarians at one of their first classes last fall.

No one raised a hand.

"You can negotiate with a terrorist," the priest said, answering his own question, as all eyes drifted to O'Doherty.

"They want me to argue," he says later, almost as if he can't believe his luck. "I can start an argument in an empty house."

His classmates told me an illuminating story. In one class, they engaged in role-playing. The three instructors hung signs around their necks and asked the seminarians to stand behind the person who most needed the support of a priest. Most stood in back of the person labeled as religious. A few stood in back of the person labeled a prostitute. Only O'Doherty stood behind the person labeled a homosexual.

Asked about it, O'Doherty shrugs.

"Hey, I was in prison. I was married. I have a gay brother. Who am I to judge anyone?"

Having been married didn't exclude him from becoming a priest, because the marriage was annulled. Neither did his past membership in the IRA. But there was the small matter of having tried to kill Bishop Tickle.

Thomas Groome, an Irish-born theologian at Boston College, explains that canon law forbids anyone who has killed or tried to kill an ordained cleric in the Catholic Church from becoming a priest. Such a sacrilege requires dispensation at the highest levels of the church. "Technically, only the pope can forgive this," says Groome, a former priest.

Tickle died of natural causes in 1994 and could not vouch for O'Doherty, but Bishop Edward Daly could. Daly is one of the most venerated priests in Ireland, a fierce critic of violence. A photograph showing him waving a white handkerchief as he and a group of men tried to get first aid for one of the casualties of Bloody Sunday is one of that day's indelible images. Daly, who was especially kind to O'Doherty's mother, had corresponded with O'Doherty and visited him in prison and believed his conversion to pacifism was genuine and Gospel inspired. Daly assured the Vatican in general and Pope John Paul II in particular that O'Doherty had the potential to become a good priest. With Daly behind him and with the sponsorship of Diarmuid Martin, the archbishop of Dublin, O'Doherty was accepted at St. Patrick's College.

The Reverend Kevin Doran, who recruits candidates for the priesthood for the Dublin Archdiocese, says O'Doherty was accepted last year with the understanding that neither he nor anyone in the church would publicly discuss his story during his study for the priesthood. Doran, in an e-mail, says: "There is, undoubtedly, a 'story' in Shane's journey to seminary. The diocese has taken the view, however, that this is not the time to focus on that story."

Groome says some will see O'Doherty's candidacy for the priesthood as a sign of just how desperate the Catholic Church is for priests. But Groome believes a defining characteristic of Catholicism is at play.

"At its best, Catholicism has great magnanimity," Groome says. "We believe in last-minute conversions. We like the story of the good thief who repented on the cross. O'Doherty's life story is about redemption, but it redeems all of us. The great saint, the great soldier, and the great lover are all similar. They are gamblers, full of idealism, looking for a noble cause."

When, God willing, he is ordained, Shane Paul O'Doherty says, he knows where his ministry lies.

The prisons.

A Gesture Life

Colm Tóibín

from *The New York Times Magazine*

Before a vast throng, the old pope revealed his inner life.

He turned like an actor turns. He seemed, as the television lights illuminated his face, to be intrigued and then mildly astonished by the size of the crowd. He seemed, as he stood alone, wearing immaculate white, to have come to us from another world, and to be bemused and surprised by the universe he now saw before him. It was August 14, 1991, at the monastery of Jasna Góra, the church of the Black Madonna at Czestochowa, the spiritual capital of Poland. Researching a book on Catholicism in Europe, I had joined a million young people gathered that day to see the pope.

The temporary altar was perched on the old walls of the monastery; below was a natural amphitheater. John Paul slowly began to walk up the steps. I cannot remember if there was music or a choir, because that was not important then. How he moved was important; his gait was deliberate and considered, but neither frail nor faltering. Even though he had his back to us, it appeared as he ascended as if his mind were pondering some deep, old spiritual hurt, something personal and sacred to him, and he had forgotten his exalted role in the world.

And then he hesitated, and he turned, and he managed a great melancholy smile while never losing an aura of power. Not once was his effect unambiguous for those hours when I watched him as the Polish night came down and lights were turned up and his face appeared on huge screens; not one gesture or shift of tone could be described simply, using a single term. His humility as he observed the crowd came patterned with pride; his burdened self came lined with real strength; the guarded image he portrayed, almost a loneliness, came mixed with a sense of exhilaration at where he was now and what he saw. He combined innocence and knowledge.

He did not wave or make any gesture but prepared to turn and make his way closer to the altar, allowing his steps now to wander from side to side as if he were alone and in a state of reverie and contemplation. And then he seemed to take in the congregation out of the sides of his eyes as he turned briefly and waved for the first time.

The ceremony lasted for hours. He did not once lose the full rapt attention of the crowd. He did nothing dramatic, said nothing new. Before he spoke—and every word he said was translated into many languages on our radios—he remained still. There must have been music. But it is the lights that I remember and the sense that he had no script for this, that it was natural and improvised and also highly theatrical and professional. More than anything, it was unpredictable.

And in that first hour, or maybe half hour, he did something genuinely astonishing. With a million of us watching, he lifted his hands and cupped them over his face. It was nothing like a gesture of despair; he did not put his face into his hands out of unhappiness. He held his head high and proud so it could be seen, and he left his hands in place covering it. The crowd watched him, presuming this would last a few moments as he sought some undistracted purity for his prayer or his contemplation. We waited for him to lower his hands, but he did not. He stayed still, the world gazing up at him. What he did ceased to be a public gesture and became instead intensely private. It was like watching somebody sleeping. I do not know how long it lasted. Maybe twenty minutes; maybe half an hour. He was offering the young who had come here in the infant years of Eastern European democracy not a lesson in doctrine or faith or morals but some mysterious example of what a spiritual life might look like. Somehow he managed to put a sort of majesty into it. Even those among us, like myself, who had no faith anymore and a serious argument with the church had to watch him with awe. He was showing us his own inner life as beautifully simple as well as strange and complex.

Then he spoke. He listed all the countries represented at the event, giving special mention to Russia's "passing from slavery." The large contingent of Spaniards kept interrupting him, singing, "Juan Pablo segundo, te quiere todo el mundo." And he managed again to seem impatient with them and amused by them also. When, in his list of countries, which he delivered in Polish, he came to the United States, he asked his audience, "Do you know where that is?" And then half under his breath, but loud enough for his translator to hear, he muttered ruefully, "Perhaps too well."

Soon there were hymns, and the pope became somber. He moved the atmosphere effortlessly from that of a rock concert to that of the solemn vigil of the fifteenth of August, marking the assumption of the Virgin Mary into heaven. A large, heavy cross was carried up the steps by a group of young people; prayers were read by representatives from various countries. When the girl from Sudan finished her contribution, she turned and sprang, frantically making her way toward the pope. She made it up two flights before she was caught by security. The crowd shouted and whistled, as the guards seemed to be causing her pain. And then the pope stood and motioned toward her. The security men hesitated and then let her spring once more toward the pope and run to him and embrace him. She wrapped her arms around him.

His sermon displayed him at his most eloquent and mysterious. The words he repeated were "I am. I remember. I watch." "Look at the cross and forget not. . . . To watch is to love your neighbor—it means fundamental human solidarity." He did not mention sex or sin. He gave his blessing in Latin and then stood alone in silence as one of the hymns known to most of the audience was sung.

I watched his face on one of the big screens. In repose he was managing still to be both the stern father and the kind uncle, allowing the considerable number of ambiguities in his being to amount to something powerful and touching and memorable. His eyes were kind and intrigued by things but also guarded, almost weary; and then, watching him there under the fiercely sharp lights that Polish television shined on him, I studied his mouth, which seemed to me that night to belong to a different being, a more implacable and more stubborn man who would care deeply about discipline and doctrine. His eyes understood and forgave everything; his mouth and the set of his chin forbade deviation and did not want there to be any change. His power, as the night came to an end, arose from the tension between the two, the lure of the drama in his own physiognomy. It is unlikely that the church in our lifetime will be able to find a figure as interesting and intriguing. It is unlikely that the million of us there that night will ever again in our lives see a spectacle so effective and seductive. The glory, or its very opposite, has departed.

Was Shakespeare Catholic?

Clare Asquith

from *Commonweal*

*Clues from his plays and hints from history point to the Bard's con-
nection to the "old religion."*

Ever since a seventeenth-century Protestant clergyman,
Richard Davies, remarked that "William Shakespeare dyed a
papist," Shakespeare's religion has been a thorny subject for
scholars and biographers. Protestant England would much
rather he had not died a papist. Three hundred years after
Shakespeare's death, English Catholics were still viewed as a
fifth column liable to join forces with the country's enemies
at a moment's notice. Even today, England's entry into the
European Union is portrayed in some quarters as a Vatican
plot to reclaim England for Catholic Christendom.

Until recently the English nation was viewed as incon-
trovertibly Protestant, and, of course, so was the national
poet. Favorite schoolboy quotations stressed his solidarity
with the Elizabethan nation-state. The patriotic concluding
speeches of *King John* and *Henry VIII;* the battle cry of the
"reformed" military hero, Henry V; the support throughout
Shakespeare's works for authority and the rule of law all

identified the playwright as a staunch Protestant Englishman. "Naught shall make us rue," as the Bastard says at the end of *King John,* "If England to herself do rest but true."

But what was England's "self," exactly—to what should she rest "true"? These lines have always been read in the light of the play's depiction of the proud reunion of the country after the divisions created by the pope's mischievous interdict of the English king—supposedly a parallel to the country's antipapal solidarity in the face of the similar interdict of Elizabeth (1533–1603). Yet in the play the Bastard's lines actually celebrate the moment England submits to the authority of the papal deputy and resumes relations with Rome.

What are we to make of this kind of ambiguity, which is so typical of Shakespeare? Many scholars see it as evidence of his political and religious neutrality. Still, there is another possible explanation, one that politically oppressed audiences such as those in Soviet-dominated Eastern Europe would readily understand.

During my years in Moscow as the wife of a British diplomat, I was introduced to the doublespeak of subversive drama, an ingenious method designed to circumvent the communist censor. Minute alterations to plays by classical authors enabled dissidents to communicate with their audience about contemporary politics. The result gave initiates an enjoyable sense of complicity but was innocent enough to hoodwink the authorities. I began to wonder whether the many incongruities in the apparently apolitical works of Shakespeare and his contemporaries indicated that they were playing the same dangerous game.

So long as Shakespeare was seen as a pillar of the establishment, no one dreamed of looking for coded meanings in his work. Today the characteristic ambiguity of his writing is beginning to take on a new significance. Since the Second World War, England has become less certain of her Protestant identity. "Is This the Death of Protestant England?" asked one apprehensive headline in the wake of the blanket coverage by the English media of the funeral of Pope John Paul II. Historians no longer feel obliged to perpetuate the orthodox "Whig" view of England's history and have been reexamining the nature of Protestantism in Shakespeare's day. Influential books such as Eamon Duffy's *Stripping of the Altars* conclude that the embrace of Protestantism was largely reluctant. This is a revolutionary position. As presented by Protestant historians, England welcomed the Reformation. Henry VIII's (1491–1547) quarrel with the pope and dissolution of the monasteries constituted a break with the superstitious past. Reformers swept away the obscurantist ceremonies and the humiliating subservience to Rome and gave the country a national church, the Protestant work ethic, the Bible in English. They released a new spirit of intellectual inquiry and national self-confidence that was to be embodied some seventy years later in the works of Shakespeare.

Recent research has resurrected a wider and darker picture, however. Fresh evidence from parish records and wills, from neglected manuscripts and archives, and from the writings of exiles indicates that Shakespeare lived in an age of silent, sullen resistance to the imposed new order. In spite of penal legislation and horrific executions, Catholics remained in the majority through 1600, conforming under duress, not out of conviction. Elizabeth's undermanned national church was still a raw, uncomfortable compromise. On a religious level it satisfied few and was implemented by force and subterfuge. Catholics were not the only casualties. Humanists and scholars of all persuasions were alienated by the narrow Bible-based ideology imposed at Oxford and Cambridge. Protestants themselves suffered. Those who objected to state control of religion were efficiently eradicated in a McCarthyite purge led by the archbishop of Canterbury. By the time Shakespeare began to write, in the late 1580s, there was a widely held view across the political spectrum that the English Reformation had been a destructive failure. It had been hijacked and had become the vehicle for the ambitions of a corrupt, power-hungry elite led by two powerful royal advisers, the father-and-son team William and Robert Cecil.

Shakespeare's biographers now give full weight to material sidelined by earlier scholars. There were many Catholics among his family, friends, and neighbors, all of whom suffered under the crippling new laws. The current consensus is that his childhood was deeply imbued with the "old religion," and that as an adolescent he may well have been involved in the 1580 Jesuit mission led by the charismatic Edmund Campion.

Few scholars, though, entertain the possibility that Shakespeare retained Catholic beliefs throughout his working life. In a recent letter to the London *Tablet,* Richard Wilson, author of *Secret Shakespeare* and a leading proponent of the Campion connection, maintains that Shakespeare was ultimately "repelled" by the extremism of the Jesuit-led mission to England. Michael Wood (*In Search of Shakespeare*) believes that by 1600, Shakespeare's "mind was too open, his habit of empathy too deep-rooted, to side with one view anymore." In his best-selling *Will in the World,* Stephen Greenblatt takes the same line: Shakespeare's mind was too free, speculative, and wide-ranging to be confined by the prescriptive dogma of the Catholic Church. It appears that the Protestant Shakespeare is being replaced by a secular one.

For centuries, though, Catholics, however unscholarly, have had an unwitting advantage over many Shakespearean critics. They possess part of the key to a forgotten form of coded writing familiar to the dissident intelligentsia of Elizabethan and Jacobean England. Acquaintance with Catholic idiom, history, and liturgy offers a glimpse of something momentous hidden beneath the familiar words, encouraging an alert reader to look beyond the familiar fabric of the work and discover a second layer below. Once detected, the concealed dimension is so distinct and coherent that there is no danger of reading in a subjective meaning. A clear political message emerges, one that Shakespeare, like an Eastern European dissident, deliberately injected into his work using signals designed to alert those who remembered the practices of the old religion while avoiding unwelcome attention from those who did not.

Shakespeare has always been seen as a writer capable of unparalleled precision of thought and language who could be—and often was—unaccountably discursive. Dr. Johnson censured him for failing to observe the classical unities, and for pursuing the "fatal Cleopatra" of wordplay at the expense of coherence. To dissidents, though, these patches of apparently loose writing had a purpose. Rather like hollow sounds discovered by those tapping a wall in the search for a hidden chamber, they would once have attracted immediate scrutiny from certain readers and speculators.

A typical instance of Shakespearean digression occurs at the end of *The Merchant of Venice*. Because of its lyrical beauty, most of us fail to notice that the strangely brief final act is almost completely extraneous to the plot. I have chosen this example because it will ring bells with Catholics who have attended the Easter Triduum. Among the highlights of the liturgy are certain distinctive elements: the Easter moon, the veneration of the cross, solemn music in the open air, a single candle, the repeated refrain "This is the night." All these are reminders of key stages in the three days of symbolic ceremony when the church celebrates the entry of light into a darkened world as she reenacts the events of Christ's Last Supper, passion, and resurrection.

Once central to Christendom, these ceremonies were banned at the time of the Reformation and, at least among Protestants in northern Europe and much of North America, are now largely unknown. So from the seventeenth century onward only Catholics would be likely to notice that exactly the same combination of elements is puzzlingly present in this final act—moonlight, a single candle dispelling the darkness, music, the repeated phrase "in such a night," kneeling at holy crosses. Anyone who has lectured on Shakespeare and Catholicism will know that this unexpected parallel is pointed out frequently if tentatively by Catholics in the audience.

The links between the Easter liturgy and *The Merchant of Venice* are striking. The opening love-duet between Lorenzo and Jessica in act 5 repeats the phrase "in such a night" eight times: exactly the same number that the phrase "This is the night" is repeated in the great Easter hymn the "Exultet." Like the Easter Vigil, the action ends at dawn and takes place on a night when the moon is full. Music of a distinctly spiritual kind induces meditations on the power of harmony to touch the immortal soul. The heroine, Portia, about to arrive home, is reported to be kneeling at holy crosses in the company of a hermit. When she enters, she is struck by the distant effect of a light burning in her hall: "How far that little candle throws his beams! / So shines a good deed in a naughty world." Trite though these words are, they express the theological symbolism of the paschal candle.

The echoes continue throughout the act. The Easter Vigil describes the stars as the "lights of heaven"; so does Shakespeare. The "Exultet" celebrates the "night on which heaven is wedded to earth"; Shakespeare's is a night when the lovers Lorenzo and Jessica celebrate a daring elopement and the newlywed Portia prays for "happy wedlock hours." This is the night, according to the "Exultet," when the Jews escaped from captivity; in such a night, says the Christian Lorenzo, in order to marry him the Jewish Jessica escaped from her jealous father, Shylock. One of the most memorable phrases from the Good Friday reading of St. John's Passion, *Ecce homo,* is recalled in a deliberately superfluous phrase, "This is the man," a reference deepened in the exchange that follows: "You should in all sense be much bound to him / For, as I hear, he was much bound for you."

Are these simply nostalgic echoes of the old religion? Or are they, as some critics suggest, instances of outdated spiritual language being recycled for secular purposes? A close look at the play suggests something more unexpected and startling, indicating an underlying artistic unity of which even eighteenth-century critics like Johnson would have approved.

One of the first results of applying the new version of English Reformation history to sixteenth-century literature is the discovery that it was common practice to use coded language to plead the cause of toleration with the queen. A delusion of Elizabethan Catholics, carefully fostered by the regime, was that the queen was secretly in favor of their cause. The private masques and entertainments at the great houses she visited on her journeys around the country were full of skillfully contrived political messages, sponsored by Catholic gentry who knew that Elizabeth prided herself on her skill in decoding allegory. The messages were all of course deniable; to plead openly for religious toleration was fatal. The unfortunate Richard Shelley died in prison merely for presenting a written appeal to the queen, and it is unlikely that she ever read one of the most direct and eloquent pieces of Elizabethan prose, *A Humble Supplication,* written by Robert Southwell, a Jesuit missionary on the run from her ubiquitous spy service. But she certainly saw the plays of Shakespeare's predecessor, the court dramatist John Lyly, who specialized in allegorical pleas for toleration, describing one of his plays

as a Trojan horse—a gift with a dangerous message. Read
with the revisionist understanding of Elizabethan history in
mind, *The Merchant of Venice,* written in the mid-1590s, is
shown to be in the same mold; it deploys ravishing language,
a gripping story, a flattering central role, partly to entertain
but also to persuade the queen to look mercifully on her suffering subjects and lift the ban on their native religion.

Only in the light of a plea to the queen does the strange
last act of the drama make artistic sense. The key to discov-
ering its inner meaning is to revisit the play with the revised
history and the Catholic background in mind, and to bring
a resolutely literal, crossword mentality to the text, staying
constantly on the alert for puns, hidden allusions, and oblique
wordplay—the approach that sixteenth-century readers, the
queen above all, brought to literature. Seen in this light, the
play's many digressions double as wittily accurate topical
references.

First, a trail of allusions suggests that the clever, beautiful, much-courted Portia would have been understood as a
flattering portrait of the queen, and that the plot contains
an ingeniously coded dramatization of Elizabeth's dilemma
as the ruler of a country torn by bitter religious conflicts.
Shakespearean scholars Peter Milward and John Klause point
out that the Jewish-Christian feud in *The Merchant of Venice* has
unmistakable parallels with the Puritan-Catholic feud divid-
ing Shakespeare's England. The Venetian usurer, Shylock,
has close affinities with London's Puritan moneylenders,
known as "Christian Jews." These would have been more
familiar to Shakespeare's audiences than Jews themselves,
who had been banned from England. Like Shylock, these
godly capitalists were steeped in the language and thinking
of the Old Testament, and like him were derided by many as
hypocrites who condemned worldliness yet amassed worldly

goods. And they were vengeful. "Puritan" Protestants loathed Catholics not simply because they represented the antichrist, but because Catholics had persecuted them so brutally during the previous reign of Mary Tudor (1553–58). Quoting Old Testament precedents, Shylock uses the law to exact savage revenge on his enemy. In the same way, Puritan priest hunters and their sponsors levied charges of treachery against Catholic priests, who were accordingly hanged, drawn, and quartered. The young Jesuit Robert Southwell, a widely admired poet, died in this way in February 1595, after three years of torture at the hands of his Puritan captor, Richard Topcliffe.

In *The Merchant of Venice,* through sheer intellectual brilliance tempered by compassion, Portia solves the impasse between the vengeful Shylock and the contemptuous Antonio. This, Shakespeare suggests, is what the equally shrewd and merciful Elizabeth can do for her country. At the end of the play he goes further. He attempts to awaken Elizabeth to the true significance of the religion her Protestant churchmen dismissed as "popish trish-trash." Stealthily, he attempts to reconcile her to the Catholicism she would have remembered from her childhood, invoking lost ceremonies that not only embodied the beauty and theological depths of the banned liturgy, but also the annual occasion during the Easter Vigil where converts were officially welcomed into the church.

Act 5 takes the form of a single extended scene, a meditative coda to the play, ending with a brief flurry of action as true identities are revealed all around. Portia's household "ceremoniously" prepares a musical welcome for her as she journeys back from her courtroom triumph, penitentially kneeling and praying at wayside crosses. The aim of her servants is to guide her home: "Wake Diana with a hymn! / With sweetest touches pierce your mistress' ear, / And draw her home with music."

Their aim coincides with Shakespeare's designs on Elizabeth. The allusion to the virginal Diana evokes the moon goddess who was the queen's most popular allegorical identity. When Portia finally appears on stage, the night-time impact of candle and music takes her by surprise: "Music! . . . / Methinks it sounds much sweeter than by day"; "How far that little candle throws his beams." She apprehends her own household as if for the first time, transfigured by the occasion. It holds a beauty she was previously unaware of: "How many things by season season'd are / To their right praise and true perfection!" These lines typify Shakespeare's "cryptic crossword" technique: the emphasis on *season,* the pun on *right,* the quietly incongruous word *praise* all pick up the previous allusions to the Good Friday veneration of the cross and the Holy Saturday "Exultet" and place the scene firmly in the context of the Easter liturgy.

The austerity of her journey and the nighttime ceremony have a profound effect on Portia. They remind her that she is subject to a greater power; her response recalls the lesson of the paschal candle. "Let me give light," she says, "but let me not be light." She is awed and humbled. In lines that gracefully recall the language of the Easter blessing of water, Shakespeare relates this newfound humility to the correct relationship of a secular monarch to God, the true king. "A substitute shines brightly as a king / Unto the king be by, and then his state / Empties itself, as doth an inland brook / Into the main of waters." Elizabeth was criticized for usurping the spiritual authority of the church and was fond of describing herself as God's deputy on earth; here Shakespeare reminds her of the limitations of her power. His prevailing tone is persuasive. In the final lines he conveys the admiration and gratitude due to a mistress who drops "manna in the way / Of starved people." The language evokes the return of the Mass, the one thing Catholics most longed for.

Did Elizabeth respond to this plea? It seems not. The plays Shakespeare wrote over the next few years are models of political correctness: it looks as if the court dramatist was cautioned, and his work suspiciously scrutinized. Even so, he managed to smuggle through artful disclaimers that would have meant nothing to the censor but that again opened out a second layer of meaning for dissident onlookers. Another of these covert references gives a second glimpse of the way Shakespeare deliberately planted markers in apparently rambling patches of dialogue in order to give a sharply political dimension to his plays.

In the first scene of *Much Ado about Nothing,* written not long after *The Merchant of Venice,* Benedick is being teased for his misogyny. As it is so often in Shakespeare, the banter is bafflingly obscure. In fact, the teasing conceals a skein of allusions associating Benedick with the thousands of "don't knows" who were beginning to regret their conformity to the state religion and to reconsider the merits of revived, Counter-Reformation Catholicism.

One joke is particularly puzzling. If Benedick ever does fall in love, laugh his friends, he will sign a letter on "the sixth of July." Benedick is stung. "Mock not, mock not," he reproves, "Ere / you flout old ends any further, examine your / conscience." Like the language of the liturgy, July 6 meant nothing to Protestants at the time, and nothing either to modern textual commentators. But to Elizabethan Catholics it was a highly significant date. It was on July 6 that Henry VIII executed Sir Thomas More, his former chancellor, for refusing to acknowledge the monarch as the supreme head of the Church of England. More had become the model for "recusant" English Catholics, ready to face destitution, imprisonment, exile, or death for their religion. The significance of the date was deepened for Catholics when the young Edward VI, Henry VIII's fervently Protestant son, also died on July 6—clearly a judgment on his heretic father. This is why Benedick puts a stop to the banter. His friends have gone too far. Mock not old ends, he says—the deaths of Thomas More and Edward are not a laughing matter—and his parting shot, "Examine your conscience," is a reminder of the case of conscience that drove More to the scaffold. From this moment on, Benedick's behavior—and the hidden identity of Beatrice—would have been of consuming interest to dissident audiences.

The Easter liturgy in *The Merchant of Venice* and the death of Thomas More in *Much Ado* are only two of the many markers in Shakespeare that have been neglected over the centuries because they depend for their impact on a history largely overlooked until now. They represent more than the lingering resonance of the old religion. They can be compared to the PULL HERE tabs on modern packaging, highlighting accessible entry points to Shakespeare's masterpieces, revealing a series of topical linings exquisitely tailored to fit the great universal plays. And these entry points lead to a second discovery: Shakespeare was not dealing in vague topical parallels. He developed a series of code words that remain the same throughout his work and give the reader unerring compass bearings to the hidden dramas. These simple code words, some of them shared by fellow writers, include terms for Protestantism, Catholicism, England, the queen, the Reformation, the Catholic powers abroad, the underground resistance. They provide the basis for a range of more fleeting topical allusions, many of them brilliantly ingenious, some of them intensely poignant.

Shakespeare's published work is prefaced by hints that a hidden layer is there, waiting to be discovered. "Read him therefore; and again and again," urge the actors Heming and Condell in the preface to the First Folio. They advise those who do not catch on to the wit that lies "hid" in the plays to consult Shakespeare's friends, the Catholic or crypto-Catholic poets who supply the series of literary tributes that follows the preface. Those who do catch on should act as "guides" to others. But, as persecution continued and Catholicism was gradually eliminated from English public life, it seems the generations of potential guides kept silent about what they knew. And, gradually, as the full political context was forgotten, so was the existence of the code.

Four hundred years later, things have changed. Now that England's anti-Catholicism is on the wane and American scholars in particular are beginning to take a searching interest in the history of early modern England, the moment has come for Catholicism to reevaluate its stormy sixteenth-century past, and for Shakespeare's hidden work to receive the attention it deserves.

A Global Church in a Globalized World

John L. Allen Jr.

from a lecture at Dominican University

A great shift is under way, bringing new voices, new energy, and a new agenda.

Editor's note: The following article is adapted from a lecture John L. Allen Jr. delivered on September 20, 2005, at Dominican University in River Forest, Illinois.

Premise

While it's almost always a helpful discipline to consider issues from multiple points of view, it's essential in Roman Catholicism, one of the most truly global institutions on earth, with 1.1 billion members scattered in every nook and cranny of the planet. If, as a wit once said, "a conclusion is generally where someone got tired of thinking," then we

Catholics need to be distance runners in the thoughtful consideration of the perspectives of others.

Let me tell one story to illustrate the point.

In August 2000, the Vatican issued a controversial document called *Dominus Iesus,* about the relationship between Christianity and other world religions. While the heart of its teaching was that the church cannot abandon its faith in Christ as the unique and lone savior of humanity, it also ruffled feathers by asserting that adherents of other religions are in a "gravely deficient" situation with respect to Christians.

Just after it appeared, I attended a workshop for rectors of seminaries around the world, held in Rome at the Casa Tra Noi, down the street from my office. In one workshop, a Jesuit theologian led a discussion on *Dominus Iesus.* A rector from Bangalore, India, popped up and said, "This document is a disaster. It has destroyed our dialogue with Hinduism, since they don't understand these exclusivist claims." Next a rector from St. Petersburg, Russia, jumped up to say, "No, you've got it all wrong. This document has saved our dialogue with the Russian Orthodox, because they have an even higher Christology than we do, and this is the first Vatican document since the council they've been excited about."

The same document, filtered through two different cultural perspectives, produced diametrically opposed reactions. Catholicism finds itself increasingly faced with the challenge of making room for the instincts, concerns, and aspirations of an astonishing variety of cultural backgrounds. Church officials in a globalized world have to be concerned not merely with how something will play in Peoria, but also with how it will play in Beijing, in Tehran, in Kinshasa, and in Kiev.

This observation does not mean that all perspectives are equally valid, which would flirt with a kind of relativism, or that the complexity of factoring in all the variables should become an excuse for inaction. Eventually, leaders have to lead. But it does suggest that if we struggle to understand why our leaders do what they do, or why Catholics from other parts of the globe don't react as we do, sometimes the answer has to be sought by seeing through their eyes.

Setting the Table

Let me offer a few rather random facts and figures about global Catholicism and try to tease out a few implications. This is by no means a comprehensive survey, but merely some basic data and observations that I hope will be useful for further conversation.

American Catholics

The 67 million Catholics in the United States represent 6 percent of the global Catholic population of 1.1 billion. We are the fourth largest Catholic country in the world, after Brazil (144 million), Mexico (126 million), and the Philippines (70 million).

Despite impressions of the United States' rocky relationship with the Vatican, much of the rest of the Catholic world believes the American church already gets too many strokes from Rome. For example, we have 6 percent of the population but 12 percent of the bishops in the Catholic Church and 14 percent of the priests. In fact, the United States has more priests by itself than the top three Catholic countries combined (forty-one thousand in the United States to thirty-seven thousand in Brazil, Mexico, and the Philippines).

As another index, we have thirteen cardinals (eleven of whom are "electors," meaning under eighty and hence eligible to vote for the pope), as opposed to Brazil, with eight cardinals (four electors); Mexico, with five cardinals (four electors);

and the Philippines, with two cardinals (one elector). In the last conclave, American votes counted for more than the votes of Mexico, Brazil, and the Philippines combined, eleven to nine. (Those three countries represent a block of 340 million Catholics, more than 30 percent of the global total.) American votes also outnumbered all the votes of Africa (ten electors).

This context is important to keep in mind when American Catholics wonder why Rome seems to be slow to respond to our crises and needs. From the point of view of many in the Catholic Church, America has been at the top of the heap for too long.

The Global South

Africa: Africa in the twentieth century went from a Catholic population of 1.9 million in 1900 to 130 million in 2000, a growth rate of 6,708 percent, the most rapid expansion of Catholicism in a single continent in two thousand years of church history. Thirty-seven percent of all baptisms in Africa today are of adults, considered a reliable measure of evangelization success, since it indicates a change in religious affiliation. The worldwide average, by way of contrast, is 13.2 percent. Islam in Africa grew equally dramatically in the same period; today there are 414 million Muslims in Africa. These numbers will continue rising, since Africa has one of the world's most dramatic rates of population growth. Along with the rapid expansion in Catholic population has come an explosion in African bishops, priests, brothers, sisters, and deacons. There are today more than six hundred African bishops and almost thirty thousand priests, and Africa and Asia each number approximately thirty thousand seminarians. In 2004, roughly twenty priests were ordained for all of England and Wales, while Nigeria alone ordained more than two hundred.

Asia: Asia went from 11 million Catholics to 107 million, a growth rate of 861 percent. Much of this growth, however, is accounted for by demographics rather than conversions, above all in the Philippines. There are only about thirty-seven million Catholics in all of Asia outside the Philippines. (A reported thirteen million are in China.) Pope John Paul II defined Asia as the great missionary horizon of the church in the twenty-first century, and that ambition certainly has something to do with the importance attached by the Holy See to diplomatic relations with China. Given the obvious stirrings of spiritual interest in China, and the reality that there is no dominant religious institution in the country, some China watchers believe an opening on religious liberty could be followed by a rapid burst of Christian expansion. If there are thirteen million Chinese Catholics today, there could be one hundred million within a couple of generations. Further, just as Latin America set the theological tone for the church in the 1980s with the liberation theology movement, today Asian theologies of religious pluralism, reflecting on how Christianity should understand the role of religious diversity in God's providence, set the agenda. We'll come back to this later.

Latin America: Latin America is home to roughly half the world's Catholics, at 520 million. Four of the ten largest Catholic countries in the world are in Latin America: Brazil, Mexico, Colombia, and Argentina. Despite its youth and dynamism, the church in Latin America is in some ways under siege, facing pressure from the so-called sects, aggressively missionary neo-Protestant movements, often charismatic and Pentecostal. Guatemala, for example, was 95 percent Catholic a generation ago; today it is 60 percent. Peru was 97 percent Catholic at the time of a 1992 national census; in 2002, the figure was 75 percent. Similar figures could be repeated in many other nations. While some observers argue that many of these conversions are either transient or incomplete, pointing to the phenomenon of the "Guadalupe Protestant" (i.e., an evangelical who still takes part in Guadalupe festivals, prays the rosary, and so on), the evidence seems to be that most Latin Americans who became evangelical at least a decade ago have remained in an evangelical church rather than returning to Catholicism.

There's a strong sense among many Latin American Catholics that their time is coming to offer leadership to the universal church. In effect, the runner-up in the conclave of 2005 was a Latin American, Cardinal Jorge Mario Bergoglio of Argentina, and many cardinals believe the Latin Americans will be strong runners the next time around.

Summary: Philip Jenkins estimated in *The Next Christendom* that by 2050, only one-fifth of the world's Christians will be non-Hispanic Caucasians. Increasingly, power and influence in global Christianity will shift with population. Manila and Nairobi and Abuja will be, in a sense, what Louvain and Paris and Milan were for much of church history, i.e., the leading centers of intellectual and pastoral energy in the church. Leadership will come from these regions, and the issues of concern to the South will increasingly become the priorities of the global church.

The Middle East

This is a small but politically and theologically important constituency. There are roughly 2.1 million Catholics in union with Rome in the Middle East, with the largest groupings in Lebanon, Syria, Iraq, and the Holy Land. These populations are in decline, as the pressures of the intifada, economic stagnation, and the rise of Islamic radicalism are driving them away. Today there are more Palestinian Christians in Australia, for example, than in Palestine. In the town of Bethlehem, the proportion of the population that is Christian has dropped from 80 percent before 1948 to less than 33 percent today. There is considerable alarm that the out-migration of Chaldean Christians from Iraq will accelerate due to fears about weak religious freedom provisions in the country's new constitution. It is almost impossible to overestimate the importance of these trends for understanding the foreign policy of the Holy See. At the symbolic level, the idea that the land of Christ might be empty of Christians, that the holy sites might become museums (like Hagia Sophia, in Istanbul), is a subject of deep psychological alarm. Practically, the Holy See worries that if Christianity disappears from the Arab world, then a value bridge between the West and Islam will be lost. Hence while their numbers may be small, the fate of Arab Christians looms large in the imagination of Vatican policymakers.

Europe

Europe claims 283 million Catholics, but in many places the practice of the faith is relatively inert; in countries such as Belgium, France, and Holland, for example, rates of weekly Mass attendance dip as low as 5 percent. This is true for all the traditional Christian denominations. In Great Britain, for example, there are now more Muslims who go to mosque on Friday than Anglicans who go to church on Sunday. Europe's fertility rates are also dropping; the lowest rates in human history, roughly 1.2 percent, have been recorded in Italy and Spain, traditionally Catholic nations. As one small but significant window into the historic shift under way, it's worth pointing out that today there is only one actual Roman among the 181 members of the College of Cardinals, retired eighty-nine-year-old Cardinal Fiorenzo Angelini. In the conclave of April, not a single Roman cast a vote, despite the fact that historically the College of Cardinals is supposed to represent the clergy of Rome. That point alone symbolizes the gradual decentering of Italy, and of Europe, under way in the Catholic Church.

In Eastern Europe, by way of contrast, rates of Mass attendance and vocations are generally higher, outside the Czech Republic and former East Germany, where Soviet-era atheism made its greatest inroads. In some places in Eastern Europe, such as Ukraine, Catholic communities are experiencing a renaissance, related to the sensation of having survived the Soviet period with new confidence and a sense of mission.

Themes from the South

Given this overview, one point seems clear: in the Catholicism of the twenty-first century, the global South, perhaps especially Africa and the Philippines, will play an increasingly important role in setting the global agenda. As this shift unfolds, as the voice of the South is heard, what themes are likely to emerge? Without any pretense of being comprehensive, I propose five:

Inculturation: Catholicism is one faith, but it has to be expressed through many cultures. Striking the right balance between unity and diversity will be a defining challenge in the church of the future, especially as a faith incubated in Europe and the West continues to expand and come of age in cultures with very different attitudes, instincts, and modes of expression. Generally speaking, theologians and prelates from the developing world will push for greater freedom to adapt Eurocentric models of worship and doctrinal expression of the Western church to their own circumstances. Further, as immigration and cultural mobility increasingly bring the South to the doorstep of the West, the patterns of thought, life, and worship of the South will more and more be part of the warp and woof of the church everywhere. Liturgy is one arena in which this tension will work itself out. These trends may push the envelope in terms of Western sensibilities. In general, Southern Christianity tends to be more spontaneous, with a much more lively sense of the supernatural—healings, visions, prophecies, possessions, exorcisms, and so on. African worship in particular tends to be heavily charismatic. As Roman Catholicism in the future speaks with African and Hispanic accents, it will also speak in tongues.

Poverty/Globalization: During the daily general congregation meetings that led up to the conclave in April, several African cardinals gave moving interventions pleading with the next pope, whoever he would be, to put the struggle against poverty and chronic underdevelopment at the top of the church's agenda. For many African Christians, the defining issues for the church are not the usual topics in the West—birth control, women in the church, theological dissent, and so on. African Catholics will of course have different views on these questions, but by and large the overwhelming majority of Southerners regard them as secondary. The truly urgent matters, they tend to believe, are poverty, war, the arms trade, HIV/AIDS, and structural reform of the international economic system. Hence as the South comes of age in the church, its focus will to some extent be increasingly *ad extra* rather than *ad intra*.

Religious Pluralism: There's a sense in which Asian Catholicism is to the Catholic Church today what Latin America was in the 1970s and 1980s, that is, the front line of the most important theological question of the day. In Latin America, the debate was over liberation theology and, more broadly, the proper relationship between Christianity and politics. Today, it's over what theological sense to make of religious diversity, meaning whether or not we can say that God wills religious diversity, and if God does will it, what does that do to Christianity's missionary imperative? In Asia, the social reality of Christianity as a tiny minority surrounded by millennia-old religious traditions such as Hinduism and Buddhism makes this an urgent, and inescapable, theological challenge. Virtually all the major cases and documents that have come through the Congregation for the Doctrine of the Faith in the last decade and a half, from Tissa Balasuriya to Jacques Dupuis to *Dominus Iesus* to Roger Haight, have pivoted on these fundamental questions. In the years to come, we can expect the question of Christian teaching about other religions to increasingly occupy the center of the research agenda in Catholic theology.

Traditional Sexual Morality: Catholics in the developing world tend to hold traditional views on matters of the family and sexual morality—homosexuality, gender, and so on. As the South comes of age, the Catholic Church will be proportionately less likely to tolerate liberal positions on these questions. For a point of comparison, consider the debate within the Anglican Communion after the consecration of an openly gay bishop in the United States. Anglicans worldwide number 76 million, but that includes 26 million in the Church of England, only 1.2 million of whom are regular communicants. Meanwhile, there are 17.5 million Anglicans in Nigeria and 8 million in Uganda, and in both places the vast majority is active. More than half the global membership of the Anglican Communion is today non-Western. Episcopalians in the States are only 2.4 million. The African bishops have declared that they are not in "full communion" with the Episcopalians, and some predict a formal schism.

Consider this comment, made just two weeks ago at a Sant'Egidio conference in Lyon, France, by Bishop Sunday Mbang, chairperson of the World Methodist Council:

> I and many African Christians are always at a loss to comprehend the whole issue of human sexuality. What really informed the idea of same-sex marriage among Christians? What is the authority for this rather depraved new way of life? Then there is the issue of this same people, who have voluntarily excluded themselves from procreation, a gift given to all men and women by God, adopting other people's children. What moral right have they to do so? Why should people who do not desire to have children go after other people's children?

Some suggest that as Africa develops economically, more relativized secular attitudes on sexual morality will take hold there as they have in much of the West. Archbishop John Onaiyekan of Abuja, Nigeria, told me some time ago that he finds this a patronizing Western conceit, as if to say, "Once the Africans get out of their huts and get some education, they'll think like us." He predicts that, if anything, as Africa's self-confidence and development levels grow, it will become bolder about asserting its moral vision on the global stage.

Islam: Western Catholics, with a few well-known exceptions, tend to emphasize dialogue and welcome with respect to Islam. Many Catholic bishops in the South, especially in Africa, take a harder line, insisting that the church must stand up for itself in situations of conflict, especially in states where Islam is in the majority and seeks the application of Islamic law. This is likely to press the Catholic Church toward a more cautious stance with respect to Islam, especially around issues of reciprocity—that is, the obligation of Islamic states and regions to reciprocate the religious freedom and the protection of law offered to Islamic minorities in the West. Phenomena such as the construction of a sixty-five-million-dollar mosque in Rome, the largest in Europe, while the one million Christians in Saudi Arabia cannot legally import

Bibles, will be less likely to pass under silence within church circles. We saw movement in that direction during Pope Benedict XVI's meeting with Muslims in Cologne, Germany, during World Youth Day, where he stated bluntly that a country that does not respect religious freedom is not worthy of the name "civilization," effectively suggesting that Muslim nations under Sharia are not fully civilized. The rise of the South will increasingly push this sort of reflection about the relationship with Islam to the top of the church's agenda.

Summary

These realities already are at work shaping the contours of Roman Catholicism. In many ways, they promise exciting times, as fresh voices are heard in Catholic debate and new energy pushes the church forward in theological exploration, in social engagement, and in spiritual expression. It's analogous in some ways to the early Christians encountering the Greco-Roman world, or the Christianity of the late Roman Empire adjusting itself to the rise of the barbarian tribes, or the impact on Christian consciousness of the discovery of the so-called New World in the fifteenth and sixteenth centuries. We are living through another of those geological transitions in church history where the plates are realigned, giving rise to new ecclesial topography.

At the same time, there's one dimension to this transition that needs to be faced honestly. Westerners, and perhaps Americans most of all, will have to face the simple fact that in this globalized church, their issues and concerns will, more and more, not set the agenda.

One kind of American Catholic, for example, might propose a different set of priorities for the church of the future, especially in the wake of the sexual abuse crisis: greater accountability for bishops, empowerment of laity, democratic and transparent procedures of administration, and a review of some questions of sexual morality. This should not be read to suggest that only Americans are concerned with these matters, or that all Americans are, but rather that Americans are proportionately more likely to rate these as top priorities than Catholics in some other parts of the world.

Without drawing conclusions on their merits, the plain truth is that most of these points are unlikely to be driving issues for the global church of the twenty-first century. In my experience, they do not come up much when you ask African, Asian, and Latin American leaders about the key challenges facing the church. This does not mean Catholics from the South always oppose these things; in fact, Asian bishops, to take one example, are known for their relatively democratic and transparent style, and often think Rome could do with a little more of it. In general, however, they don't spend a great deal of time thinking in these terms.

Understanding how the rest of the Catholic world sees things is critical to effective communication. To give a concrete example, I recall vividly in April 2002, when John Paul II summoned the American cardinals to Rome, how astonished American reporters who followed them were to discover that from the point of view of many in the Vatican, the big religion story that spring was not the American sex abuse crisis, but the Israeli-Palestinian standoff at the Basilica of the Nativity, in Bethlehem. (It was a discovery all by itself that the sex abuse story was not on the front pages of Italian papers.) There was a sort of crash course that went on over those forty-eight hours; Vatican officials finally grasped the pressure-cooker media environment the American bishops had been dealing with, and at least some reporters got a window into what the American bishops were up against.

The bottom line is that in a globalized church, America's sense of what's important, which issues need immediate engagement and which can wait, what the pope ought to be thinking about when he gets out of bed in the morning, will increasingly yield pride of place.

This reality will pose a challenge to the "catholicity" of some American Catholics. How willing are we to see ourselves as part of a worldwide family of faith, even if things don't go the way we believe they should? To what extent can we accept that Roman Catholicism is a maddeningly complex welter of different, and at times competing, cultures, theological schools, political agendas, and private instincts, the interplay among which always involves compromise, disappointment, and frustration? Can we bring ourselves to accept that the church before our eyes will probably never be the church of our dreams, and perhaps that's for the best, since our own dreams are always more limited than those of the entire communion spread across space and through time?

God's Chance Creation

George Coyne, SJ

from *The Tablet*

Religious believers have nothing to fear from scientific study of nature.

Editor's note: Cardinal Christoph Schönborn of Austria provoked an uproar in July 2005 when he wrote, in the New York Times, *that random evolution is incompatible with belief in a creator God. His remarks stirred much comment, including this article by Father Coyne, the Vatican's chief astronomer.*

The murky waters of the rapport between the church and science never seem to clear. Despite the best efforts of John Paul II and of Benedict XVI (when he was Cardinal Ratzinger), the struggle goes on to dispel myths, mistakes, and misunderstandings. Even today, disquiet rumbles over the treatment of Galileo, despite the formation of the Galileo Commission to investigate the treatment of the scientist after John Paul II realized that many in the scientific world still believed there was an intrinsic animosity between the church and science.

The commission's task was to investigate calmly and objectively the rights and wrongs of the affair on whatever side, the church's or Galileo's, the responsibility lies. However, in the almost unanimous opinion of the community of historians and philosophers of science, it did not fully realize the expectations of the pope.

There was a further attempt to ease the divisions between church and science when the International Theological Commission, under the presidency of Cardinal Ratzinger, and less than a year before he was elected to the papacy, issued a lengthy statement in which it saw no incompatibility between God's providential plan for creation and the results of a truly contingent evolutionary process in nature.

Now the waters have again been darkened, by the publication in the *New York Times* of July 7, 2005, of an article by Cardinal Christoph Schönborn of Vienna, a onetime student of Benedict XVI and a high-profile and influential figure in the church, in which he essentially claims that neo-Darwinian evolution is not compatible with the church's belief in God's purpose and design in creation. In so doing the cardinal dismisses as "rather vague and unimportant" the epoch-making declaration of John Paul II in 1996 to the Pontifical Academy of Sciences in which he stated that evolution is no longer a mere hypothesis and then proceeded, far from any thought of incompatibility, to draw reasonable implications for religious belief from that conclusion.

So why does there seem to be a persistent retreat in the church from attempts to establish a dialogue with the community of scientists, religious believers or otherwise? There appears to exist a nagging fear in the church that a universe that science has established as evolving for 13.7 billion years since the big bang and in which life, beginning in its most primitive forms at about 12 billion years from the big bang, evolved through a process of random genetic mutations and natural selection escapes God's dominion. That fear is groundless. Science is completely neutral with respect to philosophical or theological implications that may be drawn from its conclusions. Those conclusions are always subject to improvement. That is why science is such an interesting adventure and scientists curiously interesting creatures. But for someone to deny the best of today's science on religious grounds is to live in that groundless fear just mentioned.

Perhaps the following picture of God's relation to the created universe, as that universe is seen by science and interpreted by a religious believer, may help assuage that fear. In the universe, as known by science, there are essentially three processes at work: chance, necessity, and the fertility of the universe. The classical question as to whether the human being came about by chance, and so has no need of God, or by necessity, and so through the action of a designer God, is no longer valid. And so any attempt to answer it is doomed to failure. The fertility of the universe, now well established by science, is an essential ingredient, and the meaning of chance and necessity must be seen in light of that fertility. Chance processes and necessary processes are continuously interacting in a universe that is 13.7 billion years old and contains about 10^{22} stars. Those stars, as they "live" and "die," release to the universe the chemical abundance of the elements necessary for life. In their thermonuclear furnaces, stars convert the lighter elements into the heavier elements. There is no other way, for instance, to have the abundance of carbon necessary to make a toenail than through the thermonuclear processes in stars. We are all literally born of stardust.

How did that come about? Take one simple example: two hydrogen atoms meet in the early universe. By necessity (the laws of chemical combination) they are destined to become a hydrogen molecule. But by chance the temperature and pressure conditions at that moment are not correct for them to combine. And so they wander through the universe until they finally do combine. And there are trillions and trillions of such atoms doing the same thing. Of course, by the interaction of chance and necessity, many hydrogen molecules are formed, and eventually many of them combine with oxygen to make water, and so on, until we have very complex molecules and eventually the most complicated organism that science knows: the human brain.

While science cannot claim to know all of the links in this evolutionary chain, or especially the passage to living organisms, there is very strong evidence for a large degree of continuity in the whole process. Carbon, for instance, found abundantly in both biotic and nonbiotic systems, has remarkable bonding properties, and those are necessary for life as we know it. Thermodynamics works in the same way in the nonliving and the living world. Information storage and transmittal is very similar in nonliving and living systems. Life began on the earth, which formed about 4.5 billion years ago, within about the first 400 million years, a relatively rapid transition to life. In fact, the search for life's origins may be in vain. There may be no clear origin, no clear threshold as seen by science between the nonliving and the living.

This process of continuous evolution, called by scientists chemical complexification, has a certain intrinsic natural directionality, in that the more complex an organism becomes, the more determined is its future. This does not necessarily mean, however, that there need be a person directing the process, or that it is necessarily an "unguided, unplanned process of random variation and natural selection," as Cardinal Schönborn describes it. It is precisely the fertility of the universe and the interaction of chance and necessity in that universe that are responsible for the directionality. Thus far science.

Now, the religious believer asks, where does God the creator feature in this scientific scenario? If one believes in God's loving relationship with his creation, and especially with the human beings made in his image and likeness, and if one also respects the science described above, then there are marvelous opportunities to renew one's faith in God's relationship to his creation.

It is unfortunate that creationism has come to mean some fundamentalist, literal, scientific interpretation of Genesis. Judeo-Christian faith is radically creationist, but in a totally different sense. It is rooted in a belief that everything depends upon God, or, better, that all is a gift from God. The universe is not God, and it cannot exist independently of God. Neither pantheism nor naturalism is true. But if we confront what we know of our origins scientifically with religious faith in God the creator—if, that is, we take the results of modern science seriously—it is difficult to believe that God is omnipotent and omniscient in the sense of many of the Scholastic philosophers. For the believers, science tells of a God who must be very different from God as seen by them.

This stress on our scientific knowledge is not to place a limitation upon God. Far from it. It reveals a God who made a universe that has within it a certain dynamism and thus participates in the very creativity of God. Such a view of creation can be found in early Christian writings, especially in those of St. Augustine, in his comments on Genesis. If religious believers respect the results of modern science and, indeed, the best of modern biblical research, they must move away from the notion of a dictator God or a designer God, a Newtonian God who made the universe as a watch that ticks along regularly. Perhaps God should be seen more as a parent or as one who speaks encouraging and sustaining words. Scripture is very rich in these thoughts. It presents, indeed anthropomorphically, a God who gets angry, who disciplines; a God who nurtures the universe, who empties himself in Christ the incarnate Word. Thus God's revelation of himself in the book of Scripture would be reflected in our knowledge of the universe, so that, as Galileo was fond of stating, the book of Scripture and the book of nature speak of the same God.

Theologians already possess the concept of God's continuous creation with which to explore the implications of modern science for religious belief. God is working with the universe. The universe has a certain vitality of its own, like a child does. It has the ability to respond to words of endearment and encouragement. You discipline a child, but you try to preserve and enrich the individual character of the child and his or her own passion for life. A parent must allow the child to grow into adulthood, to come to make his or her own choices, to go on his or her own way in life. Words that give life are richer than mere commands or information. In such wise ways we might imagine God deals with the universe.

These are very weak images, but how else do we talk about God? We can come to know God only by analogy. The universe as we know it today through science is one way to derive an analogical knowledge of God. For those who believe modern science does say something to us about God, it provides a challenge, an enriching challenge, to traditional beliefs about God. God in his infinite freedom continuously creates a world that reflects that freedom at all levels of the evolutionary process to greater and greater complexity. God lets the world be what it will be in its continuous evolution. He is not continually intervening, but rather allows, participates, loves.

The Writer Who
Was Full of Grace

Jonathan Yardley

from *The Washington Post*

Flannery O'Connor's faith was deep and heartfelt, and she expressed it with wonderful wit.

The God whom Flannery O'Connor worshiped so devoutly put her faith to a severe test. In 1950, when she was twenty-five years old, she developed lupus, the same autoimmune disease that had killed her father when she was a teenager; with characteristic stoicism, she called the disease "no great hardship." Six years later she was on crutches, which she laughed off: "I will henceforth be a structure with flying buttresses," which, she said in the Southern vernacular she enjoyed using, "don't bother me none." Then in August 1964, she died, at the age of thirty-nine; in the last letter she wrote, mailed by her mother after her death, she apologized to a friend for not sending some short stories because "I've felt too bad to type them."

All of those quotations are to be found in *The Habit of Being,* the collection of her letters edited by her close friend

Sally Fitzgerald. During O'Connor's lifetime she published two novels, *Wise Blood* (1952) and *The Violent Bear It Away* (1960); and two collections, *A Good Man Is Hard to Find* (1955) and *Three by Flannery O'Connor* (1964)—all of which secured the high reputation she enjoys to this day. Two post-humous books further embellished it: the story collection *Everything That Rises Must Converge* (1965) and a volume of occasional prose, *Mystery and Manners* (1969). *The Habit of Being,* though, added a new dimension to our understanding of her: it gave us Flannery O'Connor the person, and what an extraordinary one she turned out to have been.

This very large book (more than six hundred pages) appeared in March 1979, a few months after I had joined the *Washington Star* as its book editor. I revered O'Connor's fiction and essays and leaped at the opportunity to read and review her letters. I fully expected to like and admire them but never bargained for falling in love with them. That is exactly what happened. The review I wrote bordered on the ecstatic:

> She was, these letters tell us in ways her other writings cannot, a great woman. Like all of us, she had her vanities, her moods, her fits of petulance and selfishness—but these only made her more human. She had saintly qualities, but she was no saint. She was a great writer who, out of a clear and unwavering vision, told stories that at moments reach the luminous borders of perfection. These letters must be counted among her finest and most durable work; they will be read so long as there is room in the world for love, faith, courage, and laughter.

Rereading these letters now, after a quarter of a century, I find no reason to alter anything in that judgment except, perhaps, to make it even more emphatic. *The Habit of Being* is a great American book by one of the greatest American writers. Meticulously edited by Fitzgerald (who died five years ago) with a minimum of editorial intrusion, the letters are not so much correspondence as conversation, between the reader and a woman who turns out to be the perfect conversationalist: a bit gabby, hugely funny, reflective, informative, impudent, wise, and—yes—inspiring.

O'Connor's life was brief and, apart from her writing and her illness, doesn't come with much in the way of a plot. She was born in Savannah in 1925, the only child of a modestly prominent and prosperous family that moved to the small town of Milledgeville when she was twelve. She went to college in Georgia and then in Iowa, did some time in writing colonies and New York City, but essentially remained in Milledgeville for the rest of her life. She never married. Her rural South and her Catholicism are essential: "To my way of thinking, the only thing that keeps me from being a regional writer is being a Catholic and the only thing that keeps me from being a Catholic writer (in the narrow sense) is being a Southerner."

She began writing when she was young and proved prodigious at it: she was twenty-one when her first story was published, and twenty-seven at the publication of *Wise Blood*. Her gifts were quickly recognized and her works were received enthusiastically, though too many critics mistook the violence in her work for "Southern gothic" and overlooked the deeper currents that flow through it. She believed in grace, the action of which "changes a character," and she understood that too many readers missed this in her work: "Part of the difficulty of all this is that you write for an audience who doesn't know what grace is and don't recognize it when they see it. All my stories are about the action of grace on a character who is not very willing to support it, but most people think of these stories as hard, hopeless, brutal, etc."

Those words were written to a woman known only, by her own insistence, as "A.," who wrote to O'Connor in 1955 inquiring about religious themes in her work and became, in the nine years remaining to O'Connor, what Fitzgerald calls an "almost uniquely important friend." To the best of my knowledge, A.'s identity remains secret to this day, which is not unusual where O'Connor is concerned; no full, authoritative biography of her has been written, because her mother, Regina, shielded her daughter's privacy with a ferocity rare (and by no means unwelcome) among guardians of literary flames.

Whatever the explanation for A.'s insistence on anonymity, it remains that O'Connor's letters to her explore and explain her Catholicism as does little else written by (or about) her. In her very first letter to A., O'Connor made the "bald statement" that "I write the way I do because (not though) I am a Catholic," and she expanded on that theme in letter after letter: "For me a dogma is only a gateway to contemplation and is an instrument of freedom and not of restriction," and (to another correspondent) "I feel that if I were not a Catholic, I would have no reason to write, no reason to see, no reason ever to feel horrified or even to enjoy anything," and (describing a literary evening to A.):

> Well, toward morning the conversation turned on the Eucharist, which I, being the Catholic, was obviously supposed to defend. [Mary McCarthy] said when she was a child and received the Host, she thought of it as the Holy Ghost, He being the "most portable" person of the Trinity; now she thought of it as a symbol and implied that it was a pretty good one. I then said, in a very shaky voice, "Well, if it's a symbol, to hell with it." That was all the defense I was capable of but I realize now that this is all I will ever be able to say about it, outside of a story, except that it is the center of existence for me; all the rest of life is expendable.

If among the other major figures of American literature there is one with religious faith as deep and heartfelt as O'Connor's, that person does not leap to mind; American writers (and other artists) are more likely to be skeptical about religion than committed to it. Yet religion never descended into religiosity with O'Connor, and it certainly did nothing to ameliorate her sharp sense of humor or tart literary opinions. When A. pressed a book by Nelson Algren on her, O'Connor ruefully opined that his was "a talent wasted by sentimentalism and a certain over-indulgence in the writing." She recommended William Faulkner's *Light in August* to A. but acknowledged that "I keep clear of Faulkner so my own little boat won't get swamped." (Later, in an essay, she memorably reworked the imagery: "Nobody wants his mule and wagon stalled on the same track the Dixie Limited is roaring down.") Carson McCullers's *Clock without Hands* was, O'Connor said, "the worst book I have ever read," but then she disliked "intensely" McCullers's work, period. As for O'Connor's fellow Catholic Graham Greene:

> There is a difference of fictions certainly and probably a difference of theological emphasis as well. If Greene created an old lady, she would be sour through and through and if you dropped her, she would break, but if you dropped my old lady, she'd bounce back at you, screaming "Jesus loves me!" I think the basis of the way I see is comic regardless of what I do with it; Greene's is something else.

Her letters, like her fiction, are suffused with comedy. She preferred typewriter to pen: "On the basis of the fact that you use ten fingers to work a typewriter and only three to push a pen, I hold the typewriter to be the more personal instrument. Also on the basis of that you can read what comes off it." She loved birds and kept swans and peacocks at the place in Milledgeville (a photo of one of her peacocks adorns the jacket of *Mystery and Manners*), but she was no more sentimental about them than she was about any of her human characters:

> I came back from my trip with enough money to order me another pair of swans. They are on their way from Miami and Mr. Hood, the incumbent swan, little suspects that he is going to have to share his feed dish. He eats out of a vase, as a matter of fact, and has a private dining room. Since his wife died, he has been in love with the bird bath. Typical Southern sense of reality.

On the central Southern reality of her day, O'Connor was ambivalent. Unlike her approximate contemporary Eudora Welty, she embraced the civil rights cause slowly and skeptically, though eventually she grasped its essential justice. O'Connor cared about people, not categories and races, and she treated her black characters with as much love and compassion as her white ones. Rereading her letters reminds me, with a force I had not anticipated, that she is one of the essential writers of my life, and that it is time to return to the rest of her work.

Confirmation Day

Seamus Heaney

from *Agni*

Examined first in catechism, passed
And ready for a blow upon the cheek
From the bishop's ring, the whole class was released
As if we were at school and this was break.
White veils, new suits, new gold-edged daily missals.
Sunlight, stirring branches, dappled grass.
In the cool porch, tea in flask lids, Rich Tea biscuits
And dressed-up parents so unused to us
And them free on a weekday we shall never
See ourselves again as we were then
And the camera caught us, in the state of grace
And turned-down ankle socks, with both hands joined.
Monsignors in birettas order us,
Girls on one side, boys on the other, back
Into line. Eyes front, one two, at a left-right lick
We march, God's rank and file, to the front rows.

The Existence of Chuck Norris

Douglas Beaumont

from Tu Quoque

Some say Chuck Norris does not exist. Here are five arguments that he does.

Editor's Note: The following was posted on the blog Tu Quoque (http://tuquoque.blogspot.com/), which the bloggers describe as "a band of existential Thomists' thoughts on culture, philosophy, science, ethics, history, politics, theology, from a Christian worldview."

Objection 1. It seems that Chuck Norris does not exist; because if one of two contraries be infinite, the other would be altogether destroyed. But the word "Chuck Norris roundhouse kick" means that it is infinite painfulness. If, therefore, Chuck Norris existed, there would be no evil discoverable; but there is evil in the world. Therefore Chuck Norris does not exist.

On the contrary, it is said of Chuck Norris: "He hath counted to infinity—twice" (www.chucknorrisfacts.com).

I answer that the existence of Chuck Norris can be proved in five ways . . .

The first and more manifest way is the argument from motion. It is certain, and evident to our senses, that in the world roundhouse kicks are in motion. Now whatever is in motion is put in motion by another, for nothing can be in motion except it is in potentiality to that towards which it is in motion; whereas a thing moves inasmuch as it is in act. For motion is nothing else than the reduction of Chuck Norris's enemy from actuality to potentiality. But nothing can be reduced from actuality to potentiality, except by something in a state of actuality. Therefore, roundhouse kicks must be put in motion by another. But this cannot go on to infinity, because then there would be no first kicker, and, consequently, no kicked. Therefore it is necessary to arrive at a first kicker, kicked by no other; and this everyone understands to be Chuck Norris.

The second way is from the nature of the roundhouse kick. In the world of bar fights we find there is an order of round-house kicks. There is no case known (neither is it, indeed, possible) in which a roundhouse kick is found to be able to hurt Chuck Norris; for so it would be kicking himself (resulting in the destruction of Chuck Norris), which is impossible. Now in roundhouse kicks it is not possible to go on to infinity, because the universe cannot contain more than one Chuck Norris. Now to take away the cause is to take away the effect. Therefore, if there be no Chuck Norris, there will be no ultimate round-house kick, nor any intermediate roundhouse kick, nor anyone's butt to receive the kick; all of which is plainly false. Therefore it is necessary to admit a first roundhouse kicker, to which everyone gives the name of Chuck Norris.

The third way is taken from possibility and necessity, and runs thus. We find in nature things that are possible to be roundhouse kicked and not to be, since they are found to be angering Chuck Norris and not angering Chuck Norris, and consequently, they are possible to be and not to be. But it is impossible for these always to be being roundhouse kicked, for that which is possible not to be roundhouse kicked at some time is not being roundhouse kicked. Therefore, if everything is possible not to be roundhouse kicked, then at one time there could have been nothing being roundhouse kicked. Now if this were true, even now there would be nothing being roundhouse kicked, because that which does not get roundhouse kicked only begins to be roundhouse kicked by something already existing. Therefore we cannot but postulate the existence of some being having of itself its own roundhouse kickedness, and not receiving it from another, but rather causing in others their necessity (and pain). This all men speak of as Chuck Norris.

The fourth way is taken from the gradation to be found in roundhouse kicks. Among roundhouse kicks there are some more and some less good, true, noble, and painful. But "more" and "less" are predicated of different things, according as they resemble in their different ways something which is the maximum, as it is written in Metaph. ii. Now the maximum in any genus is the cause of all in that genus; therefore there must also be something which is to all beings the cause of their being roundhouse kicked; and this we call Chuck Norris.

The fifth way is taken from the governance of the world. We see that things which lack intelligence, such as natural bodies, act for an end, and this is evident from their acting always, or nearly always, in the same way, so as to obtain the best result. Now whatever lacks intelligence cannot move towards an end, unless it be directed by some being endowed with the ability to kick its butt. Therefore some intelligent being exists by whom these things are directed to their end; and this being we call Chuck Norris.

Reply to Objection 1. As Chuck Norris says: "I don't step on toes, I step on necks!" Since Chuck Norris is the hardest kicker, he would not allow any evil to exist unless his roundhouse kicks were such as to bring good even out of evil. This is part of the infinite badassness of Chuck Norris: that he should allow evil to exist, and out of it produce good—the good of having something to roundhouse kick.

Tremors of Doubt

David Bentley Hart

from *The Wall Street Journal*

What kind of God would allow a deadly tsunami?

On November 1, 1755, a great earthquake struck offshore
of Lisbon. In that city alone, some sixty thousand perished,
from the initial tremors and the massive tsunami that arrived
half an hour later. Fires consumed much of what remained
of the city. The tidal waves spread death along the coasts of
Iberia and North Africa.

Voltaire's "Poème sur le désastre de Lisbonne" of the
following year was an exquisitely savage—though sober—
assault upon the theodicies prevalent in his time. For those
who would argue that "all is good" and "all is necessary,"
that the universe is an elaborately calibrated harmony of pain
and pleasure, or that this is the best of all possible worlds,
Voltaire's scorn was boundless: by what calculus of universal good can one reckon the value of "infants crushed upon
their mothers' breasts," the dying "sad inhabitants of desolate
shores," the whole "fatal chaos of individual miseries"?

Perhaps the most disturbing argument against submis-
sion to "the will of God" in human suffering—especially

the suffering of children—was placed in the mouth of Ivan Karamazov by Dostoyevsky; but the evils Ivan enumerates are all acts of human cruelty, for which one can at least assign a clear culpability. Natural calamities usually seem a greater challenge to the certitude of believers in a just and beneficent God than the sorrows induced by human iniquity.

Considered dispassionately, though, man is part of the natural order, and his propensity for malice should be no less a scandal to the conscience of the metaphysical optimist than the most violent convulsions of the physical world. The same ancient question is apposite to the horrors of history and nature alike: whence comes evil? And as Voltaire so elegantly apostrophizes, it is useless to invoke the balances of the great chain of being, for that chain is held in God's hand, and he is not enchained.

As a Christian, I cannot imagine any answer to the question of evil likely to satisfy an unbeliever; I can note, though, that—for all its urgency—Voltaire's version of the question is not in any proper sense "theological." The God of Voltaire's poem is a particular kind of "deist" God, who has shaped and ordered the world just as it now is, in accord with his exact intentions, and who presides over all its eventualities austerely attentive to a precise equilibrium between felicity and morality.

Not that reckless Christians have not occasionally spoken in such terms; but this is not the Christian God.

The Christian understanding of evil has always been more radical and fantastic than that of any theodicist, for it denies from the outset that suffering, death, and evil have any ultimate meaning at all. Perhaps no doctrine is more insufferably fabulous to non-Christians than the claim that we exist in the long melancholy aftermath of a primordial catastrophe, that this is a broken and wounded world, that cosmic time is the shadow of true time, and that the universe languishes in bondage to "powers" and "principalities"—spiritual and terrestrial—alien to God. In the Gospel of John, especially, the incarnate God enters a world at once his own and hostile to him—"He was in the world, and the world came into being through him; yet the world did not know him"—and his appearance within this cosmos is both an act of judgment and a rescue of the beauties of creation from the torments of fallen nature.

Whatever one makes of this story, it is no bland cosmic optimism. Yes, at the heart of the gospel is an ineradicable triumphalism, a conviction that the victory over evil and death has been won; but it is also a victory yet to come. As Paul says, all creation groans in anguished anticipation of the day when God's glory will transfigure all things. For now, we live amid a strife of darkness and light.

When confronted by the sheer savage immensity of worldly suffering—when we see the entire littoral rim of the Indian Ocean strewn with tens of thousands of corpses, a third of them children's—no Christian is licensed to utter odious banalities about God's inscrutable counsels or blasphemous suggestions that all this mysteriously serves God's good ends. We are permitted only to hate death and waste and the imbecile forces of chance that shatter living souls, to believe that creation is in agony in its bonds, to see this world as divided between two kingdoms—knowing all the while that it is only charity that can sustain us against "fate" and that must do so until the end of days.

Merry Sunshine

Joe Hoover, SJ

She was a person free enough to give her entire life to other people.

I found Merry Sunshine Richards in perhaps the only way she ought to be found: in Taos, New Mexico, just below the Sangre de Cristo Mountains, off a tip from the helpful clerk at the Taos Inn; after a long walk down dark streets past taco stands, art galleries, and young men throwing knives at a tree; in the middle of wondering just how stupid I was to enter a town at dusk on a bus with no place to stay and no money to get a place, and sadly contemplating a night on a park bench; at the end of a gravel road in the bottom floor of a crappy-looking apartment building, where a lean figure stood at the kitchen counter with her back to the sliding glass door. When I finally reached this place, I tapped on the glass door gently, hoping I wouldn't scare to death the figure inside. It was about nine thirty at night. She turned around calmly, as if this had been on her agenda for the day, and pushed open the door. I looked at her—gray hair, sleepy eyes, round metal glasses—and asked if she was Merry Sunshine.

Yes, she said. Come on in, she said. You know my name. You can stay. You want something to eat?

I almost collapsed onto her floor.

Other men had told me to make this journey. They were interested in my spiritual advancement, as I was a new recruit to their religious order, the Society of Jesus. We novices had already prayed silently for thirty days, moving through the house in downy moccasins, making meditations on uncharming things like the First Principle and Foundation, the Standard of Satan, the Call of the Temporal King, the Three Classes of Persons, and Rules to Aid Us toward Perceiving and Then Understanding, At Least to Some Extent, the Various Motions Which Are Caused in the Soul.

To a man it changed our lives.

Now this: Take these Spiritual Exercises and see if they can be lived. My orders, absolute and unvarnished, were to go off for a month and trust that the Lord almighty—encountered so fiercely for a month—would take care of me the rest of the time too. My directors gave me a one-way bus ticket and a pitiful amount of money, this to ratchet up neediness, and left me and my backpack at the Minneapolis bus station. I was eventually headed for a place called the Monastery of Christ in the Desert (probably chosen as much for its name as anything else), but the closest the bus went was Taos, about fifty miles away.

Who knows what will happen, my directors said. Just go and see.

Merry's place was about the size of a '76 LTD with a high ceiling. It was populated with the dogs King Henry the Eighth and Sunshine, the cat Molly, a foul-mouthed parrot named Cava de Costa. A radio powered entirely by the sun and tuned to a local station sent us Bob Dylan—"You've got a lot of nerve, to say you are my friend"—his bitter words coming off somehow lighter here. In the next room slept a man named Lawrence.

"My gentleman," Merry called him, more than once. I suspected new love. Lawrence was recovering from any number of things—booze, an old bike wreck, sleeping in the pines for months. Merry checked on him every so often while she cooked and pointed out where things were in the apartment. I just kind of sat there quietly and watched. Merry's unkempt hair, the way it framed her face, reminded me of a lion. A calm, peaceful lion, somewhat detached. Merry did not hover over me busily, inquiring about my tastes, my past, my health. Her hospitality was not oppressive. A couple of times it almost seemed like she forgot I was there. It was kind of nice. She just did what she was doing. And I don't know if there was an onion skin's difference between what she was doing and who she was. I sat at the kitchen table as if dazed, breathing the quiet air, gnawing on chicken, and liking, improbably, every song that played over the sun's radio.

Merry was intrigued that I was studying for religious life. She was almost more interested in it than I was. I tended to forget for periods of time. As I sat at her table that first night, she would say every so often, "So you're going to be a priest?" I'd reply that, well, um, yes, I was. Then she'd fish out from a pile on her table some article on spirituality, a book with a chapter about a priest, an old religious saying, and read it out loud to me. And then she'd look at me. Silence. Finally I'd say something like, "Yeah, yeah . . . yeah." I wasn't sure how I was supposed to respond. I wasn't totally comfortable being another person's spiritual pitch pipe. Maybe she didn't need me to respond at all, but just to hear her out on these things.

Merry told me she used to live in upstate New York, and after a divorce and a bad car accident she decided to overhaul things entirely. She went to a workshop at a friend's church where she held her palms up and breathed deep for thirty minutes while asking God a question. Later, in a dream, she saw mountains and a river. A few days after that she saw a photo with the same mountains and river. It was a picture of Taos. The message, to her, was clear: Go to that place and feed people. So she did.

The idea wasn't totally foreign to me. Life as I knew it—hitting my marks as a bloodthirsty mortician in the (still unreleased) indie cannibal epic *Persona Au Gratin,* for instance, or praying almost never, or just having a bank account—had also radically changed, ten months prior. I'd left acting in New York and come back to the Midwest and joined the seminary, as if answering an inescapable summons from a God who wasn't a hell of a lot of fun. Bowing to this call had been some time in the making. I'd known Jesuits since I was a little kid, by way of their schools in my hometown, Omaha. Something of them had gotten into me early on. Like fluoride in the fissures of my teeth. I never totally forgot them or felt apart from them my whole life. For a few years in my late twenties, the notion that I should be a priest stayed with me like some devoted, beleaguered girlfriend: something that was always there, that I occasionally confronted but usually just tried to ignore. I felt slightly oppressed by a God who wanted me to be a Jesuit (and back in the Midwest, I always sensed). I would rather stay in New York, be artistic and lost. Scribble furiously in tiny notebooks on the subway, land the odd film role. Act Shakespeare in noisy city parks, boys on bikes flying by, shrieking at the unpaid actors.

In the end, though, it all somehow wasn't enough. There was a twinge of the unreal about my life. There was more for me, somewhere. What exactly that was, I could never perfectly name. It didn't always make sense to want more. I was living, after all, in the riot, tragedy, and joy of New York at the turn of the century. So why leave? The line that for years lived in my brain went something like this: *I want to follow*

Christ more intensely. Sure, sure, whatever that means. Who's to say I wasn't doing that as an actor? Maybe I did more for Christ in one hysterical moment in a Dario Fo play than I would ever do as a Jesuit. Still, there was a longing, perhaps even a need. It was something to do with a feeling of inevitability, even a wild and nameless hope that I'd be very, very right for this. Something to do with knowing, deep in the fissures, that there was more in one drop of consecrated wine than in all those raucous beloved boroughs combined.

So I went.

When I woke up at Merry's the next morning, she trundled Lawrence and I out to a church to stand in line for free food. We loaded bags with turnips, carrots, loaves of bread, pasta, meat, chocolate, tiny juice boxes, and a raft of other groceries for ourselves and whoever else would come along. Merry and I went to the hospital and visited an alcoholic veteran named Little Hawk afflicted with mono and maybe TB, his lungs crammed, he told us, with black guck that he'd been coughing out all day. Merry was happy about this progress and encouraged him to keep coughing.

We went to the forest and took food to a small gathering of Rainbow Nation kids camped out there. They strolled the woods with authority, cooked and cleaned in a tidy kitchen of sticks and dried mud, yelled "I love you!" to each other through the twilight. A few just sat in a wrecked car and drank. One of the Rainbow kids came back with us to spend the night, along with two or three drunk older men. Later, a young couple in tie-dye appeared at Merry's door. They had heard of this kind lady and eagerly came inside, flushed and hungry. None of this made Merry nervous or overwhelmed. She just made more chicken. I wasn't happy about any of it. I'd grown selfish, wanted this little church and its leader all to myself. Merry started telling people I was studying to be a priest. I didn't love this either. She fed us all, and then we collapsed to her floor for the night, and the dogs squeezed in where they could.

So where you gonna go now? Merry asked me the next day. It was mid-morning and everyone else had already left. Clearly, I wasn't being invited to stay a third day. Somehow I liked her even more. As I packed up my stuff Merry and Lawrence gave me tips, kind of impatiently, even though I hadn't asked, on begging, Dumpster diving, and hitchhiking. They assumed my general idiocy in these fields, so I assumed it too and listened. Merry laid her hands on a speckled blue metal cup and gave it to me for the rest of my journey. I was very touched and thanked her extravagantly. Probably way more than the gift deserved. Then she decided to give me a little black skillet too. Then her own gray fleece. She ended up giving me sweatpants, mittens, a scarf, a towel, a can of Sterno, a roll of toilet paper, matches, candles, a sleeping bag, a pink and teal ski jacket, a pair of women's jeans, and four days' worth of food.

As I walked out the door she found, somewhere, a medal that said "Mary, Our Lady of the Roses." She put it in my palm and said to keep in touch. It felt meant. I don't think Merry said probably four words in a week that she didn't mean. It had snowed as we slept, and I walked away from her apartment past trees and bushes crystallized with ice, glinting in the morning sun. An impossible silvery wonderland: bright, cool, suspicious.

Things aren't really this way. You don't really meet someone like Merry, have her send you off in a shimmery landscape like this. I had entered a different place, somewhere out of the known boundaries. How else to explain it? Had I tried to go back, the tear in the fabric would have sealed up and all would have vanished.

My pilgrimage went on. I hitched and camped throughout New Mexico and Oklahoma. When I finally returned to St. Paul—having come to terms with, among other things, the sacred dirt of Chimayó; the beautiful boring routines of the Monastery of Christ in the Desert; a young Jesuit priest living in the desert yelling at war; a woman who exhorted me to have the faith of a backward walker (she herself once dead in a morgue and now alive, a story I drank up thirstily and still refuse to disbelieve); a man who had done everything he could to save his daughter's killer, Tim McVeigh, from the electric chair; and my big brother staring amazedly at the newborn baby he held in one hand—I wrote Merry Sunshine. These people, and others, had given me rides, money, places to stay. They were good to me in ways I did not earn and could not pay back. Altogether it was proof of something. The existence of God? Maybe it was just proof of the existence of humans. And Merry was the firstling (and the mother) of all the unstable human good that came to me on this journey, this elongated trust fall. I needed to write and thank her.

Nine months later I got a letter back. By this time I had been sent out from novitiate again. I was in South Dakota, teaching high school on an Indian reservation. One more Jesuit experiment before taking vows. Merry had lost my letter with my address, then found it half a year later on the dash of her broken pickup. The mechanic had had the truck for five months, never fixed it. A lot of things like this had happened to Merry since I left. She was no longer able to make rent on the apartment and moved out. She was house-sitting in a cabin even smaller than her old place. It had no electricity, no phone, no outhouse, only a wood stove for cooking and heat. I was prepared to hear that she had put a halt to her Dorothy Day routine and was just trying to survive.

"I've been chopping wood and have not been cooking for people," she wrote.

The cabin is ½ mi. off the main Road no one visits. I have been Really busy hitchhiking almost every day into Taos to get the food bank going. Fri the computer lists come in from the Santa Fe food bank of which Sunshine Foundation is a member. Taos County Food Bank is the official name with the IRS for my agency for the food bank. Sat or Sun I walk (if no one picks me up) about 8 miles up the hill and back (4 each way) to confer with the gent who helps distribute. Mon I hitchhike into town and fax the order. Wed I line up someone with a Truck to pick up Thurs delivery. Thurs I hike in to accept delivery—sometimes it comes on Fri. Then I help load truck and we drive 29 miles to deliver it. Next week do it all again.

In an instant my own life turned paltry and small. Such a tale does violence to my sheer *idea* of what it means to live for other people. It was enough to care for total strangers at her own place. But this! She had mentioned something about a food bank and a Sunshine Foundation, but it just seemed to me like wishful thinking. Of course she was starting a food bank. What else would she be doing?

I stared at her words—blue ink crammed onto every inch of perhaps the only clean white sheet of paper she owned— and I asked the letter, as if it were a living thing: What is going on here? What insane love brings all of this to bear? Did all the mercy in northern New Mexico get concentrated into one tall woman with an ax and little else? Or could it be that she is merely one of those people who can't sit still? A drone-ish, task-oriented person who just needs to fill her days, that's all. Or maybe not—of course not. How is she this way, and why? The gift of a car wreck and a damaged back? Those thirty minutes when she held her palms in the air? Some terrible light from the pure emptiness of the universe that took her soul and placed it right inside the souls of broken human beings everywhere? Just what has gotten into this woman?

I can't answer. Perhaps not even she can. I can only contemplate the reverberation in my own life. What does her way mean for me?

I console myself with sentiments like *We all work in different ways to help humanity. She in hers and I in mine, and everyone just needs to do his or her part, however small it may seem.*

This kind of thinking is extremely reasonable and helps me get on with my days in some manner of peace. Which means it may be pretty much a big lie. Perhaps the truth is that neither I nor anyone else, anywhere, is doing enough. Maybe there really is a call for every person to wear out his shoes and break his back feeding the poor. Maybe an extreme and reckless life serving the afflicted is the *more* I've been hunting down all this time. The one drop of precious blood I'd like to drink as often as possible. In the Jesuits, this *more* is often called by its Latin term, *magis*. The *magis* puts me in mind of Miguel Pro, illegal Jesuit priest and actor in 1920s Mexico, ducking and scurrying and ministering in disguise for two frantic years, then getting captured and shot. It could well be we are called, all of us, to exist like Pro for some kind of ridiculous *magis*. To live like the seraphim Annie Dillard writes about in *Holy the Firm*. The class of angels who love and praise God so intensely they burst into flame before their song has barely begun. In a time of war making in a distant land, perhaps out of sheer repentance nobody in this one should be living in anything more than a tiny shack with no car and no phone. Maybe burning out on a dusty road in New Mexico feeding the hungry is the only way to really, once and for all, prove the existence of humans.

Merry's letter continues:

Remember Lawrence? He lived with me at the time you visited (and gave you the sleeping bag). We all called him Bird or Birdman because he has the parrot. I have been dating him since April—went

to see him in Santa Fe where he moved in May to see a special-
ist about his seizures caused by a motorcycle crash (20 yrs ago). I
went to see him Thanksgiving. He was very shy wondering if I still
cared. My messages were not given to him by the manager of his
handicapped housing. I called 12 times. He received 2 messages.
My letters came back. At Christmas we passed each other by a half
hour. He went to Taos I went to Santa Fe. We don't have phones
or cars. Ride given by friends. I ended up camping in the Gila
Wilderness with some friends of friends. He was told I died along
the road in Arizona and called the mental health hotline 3 times at
pay phones in front of grocery store. Manager called police as he
was drunk. He's in jail with 3 assaults against officers. So Lawrence
needs our prayers . . .

Whoever said life is a walk in the park never lived in a park.
The darker side of being poor emerges. The poverty that can
so easily lead to charity (on the subway it was always those
who seemed the poorest who gave to beggars) veers into one
of its tragic byways. I hear this story and I see people wander-
ing in the dark. An absolute dark in a burned-out wasteland,
hearing all around them, on the outskirts, the buzzings and
clickings and ringings of all the things everyone else has
and they do not. "We don't have phones or cars." Prophetic
and stupid. *We don't have* . . . so we miss each other by a half
hour. *We don't* . . . and he's in a parking lot drunk and freaked
out, convinced she's dead. *We* . . . and he's in jail.

The funny part is that when I read this portion of the
letter, I couldn't help but think to myself, *I hope those two stay
right where they are.* Helpless, primitive, missing each other
in the night. Don't move an inch! I wanted to cry out. Hold
fast to the fortress, that helpless, unwired, unfinanced poetic
mess you call your lives. Oh, the hope you give! The threatened sacred habitat! The last of the last of the out of touch!
Report back on the taste of locust and wild honey! Balance

us! Balance the scrubbed, gleaming hundred million of us and hang in there! Help is not on the way, thank God! Poverty like this can be a grace, see? And there is some hard-earned grace getting churned up down there in the shadow of the glorious and surely redemptive Sangre de Cristo Mountains. Bits of that grace fly all over the place. To me, I hope. I want to be saved by association.

The problem with this kind of thinking is that Merry and Lawrence have to go through the hell they go through. Do I really wish that on them? Poverty is a grace only if you desire it or embrace it. You don't want it, try to fight it, get beaten down into it, and it's nearer to a curse. Isn't it only people like me who glorify the poor and their scrappy, keep-your-chin-up ways? Young religious types, artists, and anyone else who pines to leave the suburbs and live in beautiful squalor? What exactly are we thinking? Should we be happy for the salvation Merry and Lawrence provide by their poverty, or outraged at a society that puts them there? And am I really called to walk their harsh and dreadful road? Merry does seem to embrace the poverty she's been given; she doesn't get bitter about it, she lives gracefully through it, and life gets harder anyway. She throws herself into a makeshift foundation that, by virtue of her thumb, has to recreate its donor base every other day; she feeds all the poor people she can find; she simply tries to love a man and write him and be with him, and in the end she is ignored and passed by and presumed dead. Maybe, in spite of all her unflagging resolve, drinking from the Sangre de Cristo doesn't feel redemptive for Merry. Maybe, sometimes, it only seems like more spilled blood.

Here is the work, and here is the price. So who's in?

About a month before vow day I was back north, giving communion to a mental patient in a Minneapolis hospital. As I walked out the door, she said to me, "Praise Jesus." I stopped.

Froze, really. I wanted to say in return, "Yes, praise Jesus." But I couldn't. There were people around. I don't say, "Praise Jesus" in public. In fact, I don't know if I have ever in my life said, "Praise Jesus." It's simplistic, gospelly, embarrassing.

I think of the *magis*. My spiritual director told me that the *magis* is not always about doing a thousand wonderful things for the world. It can simply be about digging, digging down, further and further still, right where you are. And then going somewhere else to do the same. It is going to Mass and drinking the blood over and over and never really understanding what it's about. Then doing it again. It's the obedience, the chastity, the Rules to Aid Us toward Perceiving, etc.

It is, for now, a burning up of all sophistication and pride to be able to say in a crowded hallway, "Praise Jesus."

Things taste real here, in this order. As real as anywhere else I've ever been. I took my first vows. I knelt before a chalice and Host and said the words and became officially religious. I'm now studying philosophy. Hopefully I'll be ordained a priest someday. My life could be a relatively quiet one of teaching and writing and saying Mass. But rooting oneself in the Jesuits often means getting uprooted, again and again. You could go anywhere, to do anything. Even to do what Miguel Pro did. Maybe I will end up in Merry's forest someday, sent down for further studies in the reckless and extreme. To witness again a woman urged on by forces I don't even want to name. My friend is moved to do what perhaps she doesn't even understand. Something perhaps so embedded in her that she couldn't reflect on it even if she wanted to, for it would be like reflecting on her small intestine.

In the end, all I can say about Merry is that I'm in awe. In awe of this woman, not as someone whose poverty thrills me, or whose fingernails I'd put in an altar. Not as someone whose good works shame me into a frantic martyrdom. But simply as a person free enough to give her entire life to other people. If I ever hope to do the same, it seems important to just keep thinking back to how we met. To remember that when I was sad and lost in the night, this woman opened her door and took care of me. To remember standing there, heavy backpack, thin jacket, cold hands, nervous query, and a quiet voice saying, *Come on in. You can stay.*

Self-Hating Humanity?

John F. Kavanaugh, SJ

from *America*

Our controlled future will be a human nightmare.

In C. S. Lewis's fantasy novel *That Hideous Strength,* a young social scientist, hoping to break into the inner circle of the prestigious National Institute of Coordinated Experiments, discovers that the goal of the institute is to eliminate organic life. Filostrato, a physiologist who hates trees, explains to the young man why he also prefers artificial birds: "Consider again the improvement. No feathers dropped about, no nests, no eggs, no dirt."

Filth and shame come from organisms, Filostrato says. And now that we have evolved enough to separate our minds from our flesh, we can create artificial bodies to inhabit and not have to deal with all the mess. "What are the things that most offend the dignity of man? Birth and breeding and death."

Although it is true that humans can run from themselves by repressing the spiritual and succumbing to the flesh, C. S. Lewis warns us of the opposite tendency: running from ourselves by rejecting our bodies, especially our vulnerabilities in conception and death.

Our animality disgusts us—its bodily functions, its humble beginnings, its diminished endings. We are ambivalent about our need to nurse and the urgency to defecate. We long to control and deny our animality; at its worst presentation, we want to eliminate it: no more aging, no more dwindling and drooling, no helpless dependency. These are the most terrible things that could happen to us, are they not? To be diapered and cleaned by another? To be utterly helpless like an infant, like someone awaiting death? What a shame.

Our contemporary culture makes C. S. Lewis look more prescient than Nostradamus. We may not have succeeded in dominating nature, but we are becoming masters at wielding control over our own bodies, especially in how we breed and die. We are in the process of first disengaging ourselves from members of our species who are at the margins, especially if they have no brainpower. Then we can treat their bodies, now depersonalized, as things to exploit. It is psychologically easier to experiment on "blobs of protoplasm" and "heart-beating cadavers" than on a conceived or profoundly wounded human person. This change of labels will help us orchestrate our plans for "good" births and "good" deaths, for eugenics and euthenics.

The loaded word here, of course, is *good*. It often suggests perfection, full flourishing, even enhancement. And certainly our impulse to heal and extend our lives falls under those criteria. Every act of self-improvement or improving our children does. But if that alone is our notion of goodness, it collapses every good thing or act into its usefulness, efficiency, and performance.

I agree with Thomas Aquinas, who held that the good of all goods, without which there could be no other good, is existence itself, ultimately the One who is existence. There is also the good of the entire parade of species and kinds, among which are human beings, living organisms that also have personal endowments. Being a person is an intrinsic good. It is not reducible to performance or utility. Our primary response to such a good is not to use it but to respect and honor it, both for its existence and for the kind of being it is.

In this context, enhancement and prolongation of the human life span are good only if they respect and honor the good of being a human person. They are bad if they require us to reject and despise what we are.

Therapeutic cloning of beings that are human but destined for early termination is allowed in the United Kingdom. Belgium and Holland are close to legalizing euthanasia for unpromising infants. In the United States, the Academy Award–winning film *Million Dollar Baby* evoked a sea of sympathy for a young woman who wants to be killed because she is a quadriplegic. Physician-assisted suicide will be the subject of the next political battle in California. Embryonic stem cells can be created for the purpose of enhancing our conceptions and births. Preimplantation genetic diagnosis allows us to terminate embryos that have been declared undesirable, whether for genetic or sex-selection reasons.

The speculation of some ethicists who argue that fetuses and humans in a vegetative state are not persons because they have no brain performance is fed by our culture's distaste for our essential human vulnerability.

We cannot change the human genome without changing every last one of us. There will always be "the imperfect ones," unless they can be eliminated. But we may, indeed, be able to create hybrids, preferably with more efficient brains than ours. We may further weed out our imperfect brothers and sisters and prune away our imperfections. With assisted reproduction for some and discouraged reproduction for others, we may well fulfill the dreams of Francis Galton, cousin of Charles Darwin, who coined the word *eugenics* for our controlled future—but it will be a nightmare for humanity.

These are particularly poignant reflections for Christians, especially at the time of Holy Week and Easter. We are created by a God who did not shun our flesh but embraced it, even its wounds and dying. He covered himself in the shame from which we flee. This was a redemption—but not to make us invulnerable before life and impervious to mortality. It was to glorify our wounds by the power of love, and transform our death with the force of faith that God still wills, as ever, to enter our human nature. The sad question is this: Will human nature even be around to say the welcomes?

Pater Gerardus M. Hopkins, SJ

Ron Hansen

from *America*

September's end 1877,
the year called his annus mirabilis,
because his gift for poetry was discovered afresh, given inscape and leaven
by his imitation of Christ in the heaven
of third-year theology. Bridges dismissed his friend's faith as medieval, but this
calling was his solace and source, the seven
sacraments his soul's instress, a selfyeast
that could praise the grandeur of God contained
in the splendid thisness of things. Of least
importance to Hopkins then was fame gained
from writing: he sought only to be a good priest.
And in that gift of gift was he ordained.

A Remembrance of Hiroshima

Pedro Arrupe, SJ

from *The Catholic Worker*

They climbed a hill to get a better view. From there they could see a ruined city.

Editor's note: Father Pedro Arrupe, superior general of the Jesuits from 1965 to 1983, was thirty-seven years old and the superior of the Jesuit community in Nagatsuka, near Hiroshima, in 1945. This memoir of the atomic bomb attack first appeared in the 1986 book Recollections and Reflections of Pedro Arrupe *and was reprinted in the* Catholic Worker *in 2005 on the sixtieth anniversary of the attack.*

On the morning of August 6 something happened to break the monotony of the previous months. At about 7:55 in the morning a B-29 appeared. The air-raid alarm did not cause us any undue worry, since we had grown accustomed to seeing squadrons of a hundred planes flying over our heads. There seemed to be no reason to be concerned. Ten minutes after the alarm began to sound we were sure the enemy had left the city. We then resumed our usual activities in peace.

I was in my room with another priest at 8:15 when suddenly we saw a blinding light, like a flash of magnesium. Naturally we were surprised and jumped up to see what was happening. As I opened the door that faced the city, we heard a formidable explosion similar to the blast of a hurricane. At the same time, doors, windows, and walls fell upon us in smithereens.

We threw ourselves or were thrown to the floor. I say we were thrown, because a German priest who weighed over two hundred pounds and had been resting against the windowsill of his room found himself sitting in the hall several yards away with a book in his hand. A shower of roof tiles, bricks, and glass rained upon us. Three or four seconds seemed an eternity, because when one fears that a beam is about to crash down and flatten one's skull, time is incredibly prolonged.

When we were able to stand, we went running through the house. I had responsibility for thirty-five young men who were under my direction. I found none of them had even a scratch. We went out into the garden to see where the bomb had fallen, since none of us doubted that was what had happened. But when we got there, we looked at one another in surprise: there was no hole in the ground, no sign of an explosion. The trees and flowers all seemed quite normal. We searched the rice fields surrounding our house, looking for the site of the blast, but to no avail. After about fifteen minutes, we noticed that in the direction of the city dense smoke arose. Soon we could see enormous flames.

We climbed a hill to get a better view. From there we could see a ruined city: before us was a decimated Hiroshima. . . .

I shall never forget my first sight of what was the result of the atomic bomb: a group of young women, eighteen or twenty years old, clinging to one another as they dragged themselves along the road. One had a blister that almost covered her chest; she had burns across half of her face, and a cut in her scalp caused probably by a falling tile, while great quantities of blood coursed freely down her face. On and on they came, a steady procession numbering some 150,000. This gives some idea of the scene of horror that was Hiroshima.

We continued looking for some way of entering the city, but it was impossible. We did the only thing that could be done in the presence of such mass slaughter: we fell on our knees and prayed for guidance, as we were destitute of human help.

I had studied medicine many years earlier, and I ran back to the house to find medical supplies. I found the medicine chest under some ruins with the door off its hinges. I retrieved some iodine, aspirin, and bicarbonate of soda. Those were the only supplies at a time when 200,000 victims needed help. What could I do? Where to begin? Again I fell on my knees and implored God's help.

It was then that he helped me in a very special way, not with medications but with a simple and essential idea. We quickly decided to clean the house as best we could and tried to accommodate as many of the sick and wounded as we could possibly fit inside. We were able to take only 150.

The first thing we had to do was gather up extra food to provide those patients with sufficient energy to react against hemorrhages, fever, and infection caused by burns. Our young people, on foot or on bicycles, rushed about the outskirts of Hiroshima. Without thinking how or from where, they went out and came dashing back with more fish, meat, eggs, and butter than we had seen in four years. With these we were able to care for our patients.

Some success crowned our efforts because, almost without realizing it, we were attacking from the outset the anemia and leukemia that would develop in the majority of the wounded who had been exposed to atomic radiation. We can rejoice that none of those hospitalized in our house died, except one child who suffered an attack of meningitis as a result of the accumulation of fluid on the brain and died that following day. All the rest survived.

While the young people were busy gathering food, I was trying to prepare the patients in a more scientific manner to react favorably. First of all, it was necessary to clean the three kinds of wounds we saw.

There were contusions caused by the collapse of buildings. These included fractures and cuts produced by jagged pieces of tile falling from roofs. Dirt and sawdust were encrusted in torn muscles and wounds. Those raw wounds had to be cleansed without anesthetic, as we had neither chloroform nor morphine to assuage the terrible pain.

Other wounds were produced by fragments of wood or glass embedded in the body without tearing the muscles.

The third group included all kinds of burns, some very serious. When asked how they were burned, the patients often answered in the same way: they had been trapped under a collapsed smoldering building, and as they tried to extricate themselves from under it, they were burned. But there was another kind of burn whose cause no one could explain.

I asked one victim: "How were you burned?" I recall his answer: "I wasn't burned, Father."

"Then what happened to you?"

"I don't know. I saw a flash of light followed by a terrible explosion, but nothing happened to me. Then, in a half hour I saw small, superficial blisters forming on my skin, which soon became infected. But there was no fire."

It was disconcerting. Today, we know that it was caused by the infrared radiation, which attacks the tissues and destroys not only the epidermis and the endodermis, but also muscular tissue. The infections that followed resulted in the deaths of many and confused those treating the victims.

To cleanse the wounds it was necessary to puncture and open the blisters. We had in the house 150 people, of whom one-third or one-half had open wounds. The work was painful, because when one pierced a small blister, a tiny drop of water spilled out; but when one had to lance a blister that extended over half of a person's body, the discharge measured 150 cc [more than half a cup]. At first we used nickel-plated pails, but after the third patient, and seeing all there was ahead of us, we began to use all the kettles and basins we could find in the house.

The suffering was frightful, the pain excruciating, and it made bodies writhe like snakes, yet there was not a word of complaint. They all suffered in silence. . . .

After twelve hours we were able to enter the city. As usually happens after great fires, an enormous amount of water vapor condensed and descended in torrential showers. In this way, at least, the burning embers were extinguished.

Much more terrible, however, was the tragic sight of those thousands of injured people begging for help. One was a child who had a piece of glass embedded in the pupil of his left eye, and another had a large wooden splinter protruding like a dagger from between his ribs. Sobbing, he called out, "Father, save me!" Another victim was caught between two beams, with his legs calcified up to the knees.

Moving along, we saw a young man running toward us half crazed and calling for help. For twenty minutes he had been hearing his mother's voice as she lay buried under the rubble of what had been their home. The flames were already enveloping her body, and his efforts to lift the large wooden beams that held her captive had been in vain. . . .

We were to witness more horrible scenes that night. As we approached the river, the spectacle was awful beyond words. Fleeing the flames and availing themselves of low tide, the people lay across both shores, but in the middle of the night the tide began to rise, and the wounded, exhausted now and half buried in mud, could not move. The cries of those drowning are something I shall never forget.

At five in the morning, we finally arrived at our destination. . . . In spite of the urgency of our work, we first stopped to celebrate our Masses. Assuredly, it was in such moments of tragedy that we felt God nearest to us. It is at such moments that one feels in need of supernatural assistance. . . .

Apart from all these understandable events, there was one that disconcerted us greatly. Many who were in the city at the moment of the explosion and had suffered no apparent injuries whatsoever began, after a few days, to feel weak, and they came to us saying they felt a terrible interior heat and perhaps had inhaled a poisonous gas, and in a short time they were dead.

The first case occurred for me when I was treating an elderly man for two deep wounds on his back. Another man came to me and said: "Please, Father, come to my house, because my son tells me he has a very bad sore throat."

Since the man I was treating was gravely ill, I answered: "It's probably a cold. Give him some aspirin and make him perspire; you'll see he'll get well." Within two hours the boy died.

Later a girl of thirteen came weeping and said: "Father, look what's happening to me." And opening her mouth, she showed me bleeding gums, small sores on the lining of her mouth, and an acute pharyngitis. She showed me too how her hair was falling out in her hands in bunches. In two days she was dead. . . .

Of the dead, fifty thousand died the moment of the explosion itself, another two hundred thousand during the following weeks, and many others much later as a result of wounds or radiation. Until the day after the explosion, we did not know that we were dealing with the first atomic bomb to explode in our world.

At first, without electricity or radio, we were cut off from the rest of the world. The following day, cars and trains began arriving from Tokyo and Osaka with help for Hiroshima. The people who came stayed in the outskirts of the city, and when we questioned them as to what had happened, they answered very mysteriously: "The first atomic bomb exploded."

"But what is the atomic bomb?"

They would answer: "The atomic bomb is a terrible thing."

"We have seen how terrible it is; but what is it?" And they would repeat: "It's the atomic bomb . . . the atomic bomb."

They knew nothing but the name. It was a new word that was coming for the first time into the vocabulary. Besides, the knowledge that it was the atomic bomb that had exploded was no help to us at all from a medical standpoint, as no one in the world knew its full effects on the human organism. We were, in effect, the first guinea pigs in such experimentation.

But from a missionary standpoint, they did challenge us when they said: "Do not enter the city, because there is a gas in the air that kills for seventy years." It is at such times that one feels most a priest, when one knows that in the city there are 50,000 bodies that, unless they are cremated, will cause a terrible plague. There were, besides, some 120,000 wounded to care for. In light of those facts, a priest cannot remain outside the city just to preserve his life. Of course, when one is told that in the city there is a gas that kills, one must be very determined to ignore that fact and go in. And we did. And we soon began to raise pyramids of bodies and pour fuel on them to set them afire.

Eddy

Brian Doyle

from *Portland Magazine*

He was a hero: a devout youth with a lovely voice and a ferocious courage.

At about half past two on the afternoon of Wednesday, January 24, 1945, a young American named Eddy Baranski shuffled into a basement in Mauthausen, Austria. He was twenty-seven years old. He was told to remove his clothing and walk into the next room, where his photograph would be taken. He was told to stand against the wall. Probably he was told to stand as motionless as possible, so as to yield the most exact photograph. As soon as he was lined up properly with the camera he was shot from behind, in the brain, from perhaps three inches away. He died instantly. A Polish prisoner named Wilhem Ornstein then carried Eddy into an adjacent cold-storage room, where he was laid until Ornstein had finished mopping the blood from the floor. Ornstein then carried Eddy to the adjacent crematorium, where an Austrian prisoner named Johann Kanduth roasted Eddy and scattered his ashes atop a vast pile of ashes of men and women and children from around the world.

So vanished Army Air Corps captain Edward Baranski, whom the Nazis considered a cunning spy, whom the Nazis had tortured so thoroughly that he could no longer properly use his arms, whom the Nazis blamed for his role in the Slovakian revolt against the Nazis in 1944. And so vanished Eddy Baranski from the lives of those he left behind in Utah: among them his father, who never spoke his son's name again for the rest of his life; and his mother, who died of grief a few months later; and his young wife, Madeline, who had a vision of him, whole and smiling, in the Utah darkness, at exactly the moment he died in Austria; and his daughter, Kathleen, who was two years old when her daddy flew off to fight Hitler, and who spent the next fifty years fatherless, without a memory of his voice or face or smell, without even the cold facts of his murder.

In 1993, the University of Portland admitted a young woman to the class of 1997. Her name was Christina Lund. Intrigued by the university's extensive foreign-study opportunities, she applied and was accepted to the university's oldest and largest adventure abroad, in Austria. One aspect of the Salzburg program is a trip to Mauthausen, one of the many lairs of hell operated by the Nazis during the Second World War, and the one from which few ever returned.

Christina's mother, Kathleen, Eddy Baranski's daughter, decided to visit Mauthausen while she and her husband, university regent Allen Lund, were visiting their daughter in Salzburg.

"I'd never wanted to go there before, not in fifty years," says Kathleen. "But something then made me want to go, and we went, and it was chilling. I walked around. I found the place where he was shot, and I waited for something there, some feeling, some message; but there was nothing."

They went home, Kathleen and Allen, and they went about their lives, but something had changed in Kathleen, some seed opening, some cold place warming; and she began to inquire about her father, and poke her uncle John for information about his beloved brother, and write to the National Archives and to museums in Europe and to the United States Army. And slowly, miraculously, Eddy Baranski's story flew back into the world, into the hearts of his children and grandchildren, and that, says Kathleen, was his first gift to her from where he is now.

Eddy Baranski grew up in Chicago, was an all-city football player for McKinley High, and went on to college at the University of Illinois. There he joined the Army Cadet Corps, sang in a quartet, led the Catholic student group, and waited tables in the student cafeteria. One day in the cafeteria he got to talking with a startling girl named Madeline Cleary, and pretty soon Madeline and Eddy were head over heels in love, and they got married, and they had a baby, Kathleen, and then right quick another baby, Gerald, and then the worst war in the history of the world erupted, and suddenly Eddy was Lieutenant Edward Victor Baranski of the Army Air Corps, and soon the young man who had been a meticulous mess officer in Utah was an American secret agent flying into the very heart of the Nazi juggernaut at the peak of its savagery.

Because he spoke fluent German and Slovak, legacies from his Slovakian mama, Eddy Baranski was recruited by the mysterious OSS, the Office of Strategic Services, the most secretive and dangerous of the Allied intelligence units in the war. He served in North Africa, Algeria, Italy, and England (where he worked with the Czechoslovakian government in exile) before being quietly sent into Slovakia to help with a rumored partisan uprising there. In August of 1944, the Slovakian partisans did rebel against the Nazis, who crushed the rising immediately. Eddy Baranski, by now an air corps captain, slid out of his American identity altogether and became a Slovakian seller of firewood, living in the villages of Zvolen and Piešt'any, trying to find and help partisans. On December 9, 1944, the Nazi secret police, the Gestapo, having tortured residents of Zvolen for news of Eddy's whereabouts, captured him in a farmhouse in Piešt'any and took him eventually to Mauthausen. His friends in Piešt'any kept Eddy's personal belongings secret for the next half a century: a razor, a first-aid kit, a prayer book.

In May of 1945, a German citizen named Werner Muller dictated an extraordinary document to an Australian lieutenant named Danny Hunter. Muller, who spoke English, French, and Italian, had been an interpreter for the Wehrmacht, the Nazi army, under Heinrich Himmler. Ordered to Mauthausen in October of 1944, Muller was to help with the interrogations of Allied prisoners. When Mauthausen was freed, in May of 1945, Danny Hunter wrote down Muller's account of his months in hell. Muller remembered one prisoner above all: Eddy Baranski.

Eddy and his radioman, Daniel Pavletich, had both been imprisoned and questioned first in Bratislava, where they told the Nazis they were American fliers. "On arrival in Mauthausen, Pavletich was interrogated without incident," remembered Muller, but Baranski was a different story. "Since this fellow seems to be so very clever," said the Kommandant, "he deserves special treatment. This one we will hang."

"When Baranski saw [Nazi officers] all crowded in the room and the chain over the table," remembered Muller, "he turned to me smiling and said, 'I know what they are going to do now.'"

"They tied his hands behind his back," remembered Muller, "and attached his wrists to the chain above, which they drew upward. Although he must have been suffering terrible pain, he kept himself wonderfully. The Kommandant did not seem to like that and said, 'I think the fellow still enjoys himself.' They pulled his legs down so his whole weight was hanging on his arms. In the end he couldn't stand it any longer. He cried and begged to be let down, but the Kommandant insisted on keeping him suspended in that dreadful position. My eyes were filled with tears. Baranski started praying, and the Kommandant asked me what he was saying, and when I told him, he and the other officers laughed. In the end, however, they let him down."

"His prayers," says Eddy's daughter, Kathleen, "that's my father's second gift to me. At the very end of his tether, he prayed. To hear the depth and breadth of his faith, to know that now, after not knowing that for fifty years—that is a gift."

"He was completely broken," remembered Muller. "His poor hands looked dreadful. He was offered some water, but he had to hold it himself, which he was incapable of doing with his hands. It was a terrible sight, how he tried at first to sip some water with the bottle held between his arms. This was the most dreadful half hour I have ever been through in my life, and I was ashamed to be there."

And Muller remembered one more detail: before Eddy Baranski and ten American men and four British men and one Slovakian woman were executed naked in the basement with the fake camera, Muller offered Baranski a cigarette, and Eddy began smiling again.

In August of 1999, Kathleen Baranski Lund and thirty of her family and friends were honored guests of the American embassy in Bratislava, where her father had been interrogated by the Nazis. They visited Zvolen, where her father had landed in a B-17 to begin his secret mission in Slovakia, and where the president of Slovakia dedicated a monument to Eddy Baranski and his fellow Allied soldiers who aided the 1944 rebellion against the Nazis. They went to Banská Bystrica, where Eddy Baranski is honored in a museum dedicated to the Slovak uprising of 1944. They went to Piešt'any, where Eddy was captured, and they went to the house where he was captured, and there they met Maria Lakotova, who wept when she remembered Kathleen's father singing lullabies to her at night when she was a toddler in that house. And finally they went to Mauthausen, and they prayed, and a priest friend celebrated a quiet Mass at the place where so many thousands of souls fled the earth, and then they went home.

"Your father used to sing to me at night," Maria Lakotova told Kathleen. "He would hold me on his knee and sing and sing. He was so kind, and he had such a lovely voice. But many years later I realized that he was not singing to me. He was singing to you, Kathleen, to his little girl far away."

"His songs," says Kathleen, "his songs are his final gift to me. It's like I am finally hearing them after fifty years. I finally found my father. Now I know he never gave up, and he prayed, and he sang, and now he's part of me like he never was, not for fifty years. No one ever talked about him again after he died, so I never had a father at all. But now I do. Now I'll have my dad forever and ever. It's not sad. It's joyous. It's a miracle."

In 2004, Oregon's Catholic university, the University of Portland, admitted a young woman to the class of 2008. Her name is Noel Peterson. She is from Shadow Hills, California. She wants to major in engineering. She has a quick wit and a shy smile and lives in Shipstad Hall. Her mother is Natalie Baranski Peterson. Her grandmother is Kathleen Baranski Lund. Her great-grandfather was a most remarkable young man, a devout youth with a lovely voice and a ferocious courage and an irrepressible belief that his brains and energy and creativity and, finally, his life could be brought to bear to destroy a foul empire that sought to enslave the world. His name was Eddy Baranski, and his story will never die again.

Under the Apricot Trees

Sandra Scofield

from *America*

Frieda made choices, and she paid the price.

My mother, my father, my little sister, and I were living with
my widowed grandmother, Frieda Hambleton, in her house
in a poor neighborhood of Wichita Falls, Texas. We were
crowded, but it was what I had always known, and I was
happy.

Then she built a house on Grant Street, in the developing
part of the city, on the very edge of the prairie. I thought we
would go with her; instead, we moved across the tracks past
a Pig Stand Drive-In into county housing. Our duplex was ill
furnished, but here my deeply religious mother could set up
an altar and hang devotional pictures.

In Frieda's Lutheran house, we had said our prayers in a
bedroom with the door closed.

We couldn't have moved with Frieda anyway, because
she lived in the new house with a man, Collins Hamon. She
called him by his last name, in the manner of mill workers,
policemen, and nurses. They both worked at mills—she
packed flour; he packed feed—and they had been friendly

for a while, but none of us had ever met him. And though I now remember him vividly, because he behaved in a way I had never seen a man behave, the memory was dormant for fifty years, until, a long time after Frieda's death in 1983, I began reflecting on certain aspects of her life.

I was interested in learning about the Grant Street house because it was the house I had thought of as home base for nearly thirty years, and for most of that time I had depended on my grandmother for her unconditional love. Facts are a scaffold for narrative, and though I didn't know it yet, I was searching for my grandmother's story. From public records, and much to my surprise, I learned that Collins Hamon bought the Grant Street property in 1949 for five thousand dollars and transferred ownership to Frieda in January 1953 for one dollar. (This is not to say that he gave her the house. Records also show that she paid the mortgage from 1953 to 1979.)

I always thought my grandmother had the house built, but what I saw must have been a nearly completed house on which she and Hamon did finish work. He had probably been living in it like a squatter; rough men often need few amenities. As the house took final shape, it became her house. I was with her when she planted rosebushes in front of the house and two apricot trees near the back property line. This is my last house, she said; her first house had been emptied by her husband's sudden death and by poverty, and she had been split from her children for three years.

I went to Grant Street on Saturdays and was home again by dark. Frieda had a TV (we did not), and magazines, and paper for my drawings. Sometimes we drove to my great-grandparents' farm, in Devol, Oklahoma, for a few hours. Other times we did small chores, like the laundry. I folded clothes while I told Frieda about school. Were Hamon's clothes there? I don't think so. I don't think I would forget something so odd, so thrillingly repulsive.

He went in and out of the house a lot, banging doors. I didn't think Frieda liked him and I didn't understand why he was there, but it would never have occurred to me to ask. I didn't know if they were married, or wonder about it. Adults did what they did and children fit in around them.

She had been widowed since 1936 and was still young, but I think in time she became ashamed of the choice she had made, and her shame turned to bitterness, as grief had done before. Now my writer's mind runs freely over their history: Meetings with friends from the mills. The flattery of his attention. Maybe his look that suggested things she wanted—not vulgar things, but intimacies.

Now and then his daughter, C., was at the house when I was. She was twelve years old, a polite and pleasant girl. We were too old for play and found nothing to talk about. Usually she studied or read.

She kept her head down. Soon I learned why.

Her father, Hamon, beat her. I remember the first time I was there when it happened. I was at the kitchen table. I heard his harsh voice, her yelps, and then he stormed through the kitchen pushing her ahead of him outside as she whimpered that she was sorry, so sorry. I looked through the window and I saw that he had taken her to the far end of the large back lot, by the alley near my grandmother's apricot trees. He swung his arm around and hurled it hard against her back, and she twisted away, then tumbled to the ground.

I didn't think he would hit me, but he was a frightening, monstrous man, and I rushed to find my grandmother. She was in the spare bedroom changing the sheets.

Did you forget I was here? Why didn't you come get me? I cried.

And I asked, What did she do so bad? Why is he hurting her? Aren't you going to do anything?

Frieda pulled me into the bedroom and shut the door. She stood behind me and put her arms around me until my breathing was regular again. She was a hard-muscled, skinny woman who lifted fifty-pound bags of flour every day.

She turned me around to face her: It's none of our business. You hear?

That was her way of saying I shouldn't talk or worry about it. (A father beats his child.) She would always protect me. But it was not up to her to protect C.

I never said anything to my mother about these incidents. I added C. to my prayers at daily Mass before school.

Once C. screamed at him: I hate you! She ran, if you can call it that, but Hamon, snorting with menace, was always between her and an exit door. She darted about the house while he feinted and grabbed at her and finally, inevitably, caught her blouse at the back. She wrenched away, and I heard the ripping of the blouse as he tore it off her body. My grandmother and I stood in the doorway of her bedroom like people waiting out a tornado.

Hamon was gone from the house in seven or eight months, and they were divorced soon after. It was as if he had never existed.

When my grandmother planted her trees, I imagined myself checking the apricots on the trees, watching for the warm colors as they ripened. I imagined myself carrying them in my apron to the kitchen. But I don't think I ever went near the trees. Frieda made wonderful fried pies stuffed fat with stewed fruit, and I liked them and ate them, but I think I could do this only because the golden crusts and the oozing apricots were so far removed in time and form from the trees and the girl with her father.

Hamon never hit C. in the face, but her arms were bruised the color of eggplants. I saw him pull his arm back with savage deliberation and swing hard against her body. Once this happened in the house, and she thudded against a doorjamb and her eye swelled shut. My grandmother drove her home, then me.

C. lived with her dead mother's parents, and they were able to go to court to stop her father from seeing her. She disappeared from my grandmother's house and from my life.

In the 1964–65 school year, I lived with my grandmother and taught at the Catholic school where I had once been a student. One Sunday we saw in the newspaper that C. had married a doctor. Frieda said she was very happy for her. Hamon had long ago left Wichita Falls, had probably killed himself drunk in a car by now, she said. (In fact, he died many years later in California.)

Time passed, and I was much older than Frieda had been that year and I began thinking about her life in a certain way. I wondered why she would marry someone she did not love and overlook his brutality toward his child. I told myself that it was something about the times, when many parents kicked their children or beat them with belts and fists and sticks and almost no one interfered, not kin or neighbor, church brethren or the law. I'm sure my grandmother believed she had no right. I have considered that she might have been afraid of him. These explanations have not much put my mind at ease. She was a woman who much loved children, and yet she had cared nothing about C.

I didn't think until recently that Hamon was a man with strong arms, and that the house he helped Frieda finish would be her home until her death; or that she might not have been able to buy the house on her own. I didn't think until now about the times my hapless uncle lived in her house, or the times that I did, or the two years after my mother died when she rented that house so that she could live with me in Odessa while I finished high school.

All the times she would have said: Thank God I have my house.

I didn't think until recently that from the beginning she might have meant to use Hamon, and that it might have surprised her to see how much it cost her to do so. I wonder if it has turned out to be part of my mission to do the tally for her, because I loved her and wasn't guilty of her sins, but only of my own. I am sure that God knows that she was once young and happy, and that she lost her happiness cruelly through no one's fault, and where there had once been joy and faith and hope, anger and pragmatism took cold hold. It isn't my place to judge my grandmother, or to forgive her, or to try to balance that strange year against her suffering and her good acts. She failed that girl, but I believe in God's mercy; and as we must seek the right path and do the right things, we must also look inside ourselves for all the ways we are not what we should be, or even who we think we are. I am a writer because I believe there is a kind of word that takes us into the human heart and lays it bare, and I think it is a life's work to find a way to speak it.

God knows more about Frieda than any of us can know, and about other women who have stood at graves and at the doors of empty houses. God also knows that I will try to tell her story for no one's saving but my own; and I will pray for her soul, and for theirs, and for mine as well.

The Truth about the Crusades

Robert P. Lockwood

from *This Rock*

Or, how the church did not *drive Europe into a barbaric war of aggression against a peaceful Islamic world*

Back in my salad days when I gave talks on anti-Catholicism to various groups, I would always begin with a little theatrics—particularly when it was a non-Catholic audience.

Just before I would start, I would take out my wallet, pull out a five- or ten-dollar bill—depending on what I had left after my kids raided the Lockwood till—and, with exaggerated flair, place it on the podium. "I'll explain this later," I'd say, and begin my presentation.

During the course of the question-and-answer session, as soon as someone from the audience raised the Crusades, Galileo, the Inquisition, or the "silence" of Pope Pius XII in the face of the Holocaust, I'd pick up the bill. I would then say that I had planned to donate the money to the sponsoring organization if I had managed to get through an evening without someone raising one of those topics that have become traditional excuses for anti-Catholicism.

The myths surrounding these events are Catholic urban legends. Part of the reason for the persistence of anti-Catholicism in our culture is the historical legacy of the post-Reformation world. Myths, legends, and anti-Catholic propaganda created in the bitterness of theological, national, and cultural divisions in the centuries after the Reformation have colored our understanding of the past and are often used in the present as a club against the church. Our understanding of the world in which we live and the events of the past that helped to shape it is often determined by this anti-Catholic legacy.

The Catholic urban legend of the Crusades is of a ruthless, intolerant church driving Europe into a barbaric war of aggression and plunder against a peaceful Islamic world. As the common portrait paints it, the Crusades, led by mad preachers and manipulating popes, were church-sponsored invasions of a peaceful people that descended into slaughter in Jerusalem, the persecution of European Jews, and papal manipulation that led to the sack of Constantinople.

The Crusades, of course, are a far more complicated series of events in history than portrayed in anti-Catholic rhetoric. But any serious historian of the Crusades—no matter what his or her perspective—would agree that a few prejudices can be addressed.

Catholic Urban Legend: The Crusades were unwarranted European invasions of an innocent Islamic people.

This claim was never part of general European or Islamic understanding until the Ottoman Empire painted the Crusades as eleventh-century colonialism to stir up Islamic nationalism as its dynasty was dying in the nineteenth and early twentieth centuries. The reality is that the Crusade announced by Pope Blessed Urban II in 1095 was the answer to an urgent plea from Constantinople for Western assistance against an Islamic invasion from the Seljuk Turks.

Islam, springing from Arabia, had been militarily aggressive for centuries, conquering Jerusalem in AD 638 and most of northern Africa by 700. In 711, Spain was occupied, and it was not until the victory of Charles Martel at Tours and Poitiers in 732 that the Islamic advance in western Europe ended. Constantinople was able to maintain the Eastern Empire, through it was stripped over the centuries of Syria, Palestine, and North Africa by the military advance of Islam. Over the next three centuries, the empire would recover somewhat, though it would never be able to reclaim the Holy Land itself.

By the eleventh century there were three different centers of Arab rule—in Spain, Egypt, and Iran/Iraq—with the Fatimid dynasty of Egypt exercising control over Jerusalem. At the same time, there were any number of Islamic rulers with their own military forces, dynasties, feuds, and battles for power. By 1027, the Eastern emperor had negotiated relief for the Christians of Jerusalem, and pilgrimages from Europe to the holy sites had resumed. However, the rise of the Muslim Seljuk Turks shortly thereafter would destroy this peaceful interlude and be a direct cause of the First Crusade.

The Seljuk Turks quickly overran Armenia, and the entire Anatolian peninsula was threatened. Imperial forces were destroyed at the battle of Manzikert in 1071, considered the greatest defeat in the history of the Eastern Empire. Ten years later, Alexios Komnenos took over the imperial throne when it appeared that the entire empire was on the verge of collapse. Through negotiations and careful manipulation of Islamic disunity, he was able to survive and to rebuild a base of power against the Seljuks.

As part of his plan, Alexios also mended fences with the papacy, and it appeared that the Schism of 1054, between the church in the West and the church in the East, could be healed. He developed a cordial relationship with Pope Urban II, who held a council of the church in 1095 at which representatives of the empire were in attendance. In desperate need of soldiers, they begged for assistance from the West to fight the Seljuk advance. In November 1095, at a church council in Clermont, France, Urban issued the formal call for a Crusade to rescue Eastern Christendom from Islamic invasion and recover the Holy Land to make it safe for pilgrimage.

On July 15, 1099, nearly two years after they began to fight their way to the Holy Land, the crusaders successfully took Jerusalem. The papal legate who had accompanied them, however, had died. Without his restraint that had been evident throughout the march to Jerusalem, the crusading army—which had been reduced from about thirty thousand to twelve thousand by battle, heat, and a lack of water—stormed the walls and engaged in a general slaughter of the population. This was not uncommon at the time. If a city staunchly resisted an attack, slaughter was almost inevitable once the defenses were breached. When the Muslim leader Saladin retook Jerusalem in 1187, his response was more charitable and so out of the ordinary that it became legendary. After negotiations, instead of slaughter, the wealthiest were allowed to buy their freedom. Those who could not—men, women, and children—were sold into slavery. Such were the times.

Why did Urban support the idea of a Crusade to the Holy Land? The return of the Holy Land and the defense of the Christian communities under siege in the Near East were his primary objectives. But there was an additional concern.

There was the direct threat of an Islamic advance into Europe. If Constantinople fell, Charles Martel's victory at Tours would be rendered in vain, and all eastern Europe would be wide open to Islamic advance. And exactly that took place once Constantinople fell to Islam in the fifteenth century.

Why did the Crusades happen? They were not church-ordered attacks on an innocent people. They were a direct response to the invasion of the remnant Byzantine Empire by the Seljuk Turks.

Catholic Urban Legend: The Crusades were an exercise in church-inspired anti-Jewish riots throughout Europe.

Anti-Jewish riots took place in a swath of the Rhineland, not throughout Europe, and primarily in a very limited period before the First Crusade began. These riots were not instigated or preached by the church. In fact, church leadership worked mightily to save Jewish lives.

The anti-Jewish riots began with a leaderless mob prior to the First Crusade. In the Rhineland disparate groups of peasants and townsfolk proclaimed themselves ready to march to Constantinople to fight Islam. They quickly descended into violence and began to launch attacks on the Jews locally. The bishop of Speyer managed to protect most of the Jews, but at Worms there was greater violence. The bishop opened up his home to protect the Jewish community, but the mobs broke in and slaughtered them. At Mainz, another slaughter followed in this ragtag army's wake. As the army approached Cologne, Jews were hidden in Christian homes, and the archbishop was able to protect most of them. At Trier, most of the Jewish community was protected in the archbishop's palace.

The attacks on Jews in the Rhineland took place despite the constant intervention of church authorities on behalf of the Jews. Eventually, Christians and Turks destroyed the peasant armies.

When the Second Crusade was preached, St. Bernard of Clairvaux went to the Rhineland to stamp out any anti-Jewish riots, and they ceased.

Catholic Urban Legend: The sack of Constantinople took place under the indirect orders of Pope Innocent III as a means to recapture Byzantine Christianity for the Western Church.

Elected in 1198, Pope Innocent III dedicated his pontificate to recapturing Jerusalem, which had been lost to Saladin. He negotiated with the Eastern emperor Alexios III, who had ascended the imperial throne in 1195 after overthrowing (and blinding) his brother, for a healing of the schism and a joint effort to reclaim the Holy Land.

But virtually from the start Pope Innocent III lost control of the endeavor. The French barons leading the Crusade planned to sail directly to the Holy Land and bypass Constantinople. Transportation was secured with Venice, but when the time came, a much smaller army assembled in Venice than had been planned. The Venetians wanted to be paid for the fleet they had constructed for a much bigger invasion, and finally it was decided that the crusaders could start to make good on the cost by subduing for the Venetians the rebellious city of Zadar, on the Dalmatian coast. The problem was that Zadar was Catholic and under the control of a Catholic crusading king whose lands the pope had pledged to protect. When Zadar was attacked, an outraged Pope Innocent excommunicated the crusaders.

Eventually the French crusaders were reconciled to the church, and it seemed the Crusade was finally ready to embark. Then the son of the emperor deposed by Alexios III entered the picture. This young Alexios hoped to regain the throne taken from his father by his uncle. He assured the crusaders that they would be greeted in Constantinople as liberators if they helped him. Young Alexios would pay the crusaders what they still owed the Venetians and supply them with all they needed to proceed to the Holy Land if they would take Constantinople and place him on the throne. Innocent called on the crusaders to move on Palestine and forget any interference in Christian Constantinople. He thought little of the young Alexios and warned the crusaders against attacks on fellow Christians.

In June 1203, the Venetians and the French crusaders, along with young Alexios, arrived at the gates of Constantinople. Alexios had assured them that Constantinople would rise up in his favor. That did not happen. His uncle did flee, his father was restored to the throne, and Alexios would corule with his father as Alexios IV. But he found a treasury that could not pay off the Venetians. In February 1204, he was deposed and killed by the citizens of Constantinople. The crusaders saw that revolution as a direct attack on them, and any plans to continue on to the Holy Land were abandoned. The French and the Venetians poured into the city, and plunder and murder became the order of the day. Constantinople would survive, but it would fall completely to Islamic invasion in 1453.

No serious historian of the Crusades would argue that Pope Innocent III brought about or wanted the sack of Constantinople, but that Catholic urban legend remains. It flies in the face of the simple fact that the crusaders paid little mind to a pope far away when there was plunder nearby, and that the pope explicitly begged them not to attack Constantinople. Though some argue that Pope Innocent III was privately pleased at the turn of events that would bring Constantinople back under Latin control, there is nothing in his actions that would lend credence to this. Three times he warned the crusaders not to travel to Constantinople; he incessantly warned against any attack on Christians; and he complained bitterly after the fact about the ruin of the city.

Catholic urban legends always have an anti-Catholic moral. The moral of the Catholic urban legend of the Crusades is that the Catholic faith promotes zealotry, which leads only to intolerance and violence—"Just look at the carnage and bigotry associated with the Crusades."

No real historian would make that case. There is no simplistic history of the Crusades that lends itself to secular, anti-Catholic moralizing. Historians have disagreed and will disagree in interpreting the Crusades and their impact on European and Islamic life. But they would agree that we could do without the Catholic urban legends surrounding them. Like most Catholic urban legends, they are propaganda disguised as history.

The Reality of Torture

Martin Flanagan

from *The Age*

The war on terror reawakens old arguments for an abhorrent practice.

Torture—to me, the most repugnant of all human practices—is coming back into intellectual fashion. I realized this recently when I saw an advertisement for an Oxford University Press book bringing together "an array of social experts to debate the advisability and implications of maintaining the absolute ban on torture."

Next to that ad was one for a book on dance music from the 1940s. Above it was an ad for a history of Latin as a language. And there was the Oxford ad, utilizing a tone of high reason and invoking the authority of social experts, for a book admitting the possibility that torture was okay.

That advertisement would not have appeared five years ago. Something's changed. The something is us.

If I state clearly what I mean in this essay, at some point I will be called irrational. If I go on about it long enough, I may well be called other things as well. Persistent anti-slavery campaigners in the United States prior to the Civil

War were termed "morbid." In a lifetime of going to church, Mark Twain's mother never once heard slavery attacked from the pulpit. Lincoln summarized the absurdity of the legislative position when he said that Northerners didn't talk about slavery in their legislature because it wasn't their business, and they didn't talk about it on their visits to the Southern legislature because it wasn't their place.

The so-called superrealists among us will say that torture has ever been among us and ever will be. Perhaps. And there may be nothing I can do about that. But I do have some small say in what passes for civilized discourse. Never in my adult life have I felt my understanding of that term collapse beneath me as it did when I came across the advertisement for a book on torture.

Like so much in our changed world, the return of torture into intellectual fashion dates back to September 11, from which arose, among much else, the "ticking bomb" argu-ment: A terror suspect has set a bomb that is about to go off. Unless you find out where, innocents will be killed and injured. Is torturing the suspect wrong?

This is a tabloid argument. It reduces the murky swirling morality of places like Abu Ghraib to one enormously simple and attractive proposition. I don't believe torture is that simple. For example, what if the suspect refuses to speak? Is it permissible, as happens in some countries, to torture a member of the suspect's family in front of them? If Western democracies abandon what the *Economist* magazine has called their "taboo" on torture, where exactly does the new limit to behavior lie? And why?

I also have a continuing problem with the word *terrorist*. I am not denying the presence of people in the world so consumed by their mission to destroy that they will harm others without thought of human consequence. But this debate demands far greater precision, since the word *terrorist* is now commonly used to mean anyone who takes up arms against a state, regardless of political causes.

I will explain myself by outlining the case of a largely forgotten man exiled to these shores from his native land in 1849 after leading an armed uprising against the great imperial power of the day. I regard this man, William Smith O'Brien, as the champion of my people, the starving poor of Ireland, a million of whom died during these years or emigrated or, like my forebear, stole to feed their families and were transported as convicts to Tasmania.

O'Brien was not a violent radical. Educated at Harrow and Cambridge, he was a unique expression of the old European aristocratic culture. He was fond of Queen Victoria. But he also stood in direct descent from the last king of Ireland and was highly mindful of the fact. For twenty years, he was a conscientious member of the House of Commons, applying himself to issues ranging from the transportation of convicts to slavery, which he steadfastly opposed.

He sought to address the problems of Ireland through the imperial parliament while seeking to counter the violent tendencies in the nationalist movement back in Ireland. Time and again, he rose in the house to ask questions of government policy. He demanded the Irish famine be treated as a national calamity like war and bitterly attacked the English government's habit of addressing the horror in terms of laissez-faire economic theory.

Eventually, faced with scenes of mass suffering in Ireland and despairing of parliament, he sought help from the government of France—in the popular imagination of the day, England's enemy. When he returned, he said he would not take up arms to free Ireland but would defend existing rights. Further rights were taken away. The uprising he led was short-lived and futile. O'Brien was sentenced to be hanged, drawn, and quartered, the sentence being commuted to exile to Australia.

O'Brien's story shows how a decent man can become embroiled in political violence. His captivity was structured so that no one spoke to him but an official. His diaries record his losing battle to keep his mind from turning inward. He believed he was being tortured—though his experience on Maria Island in 1849 was a holiday camp compared with that of the other convicts there and with what we now know about Guantánamo Bay and the prisons of Iraq.

The ticking bomb argument works only if we all agree on what the word *terrorist* means. Globally, we don't. Politically, this doesn't really matter—countries, individually and in groups, have decided the issue for themselves—but what is being argued for here is more than a political imperative. When we discuss a subject as humanly extreme as torture we go beyond national borders and aim for truths of a larger or higher kind—what used to be called universal truths.

And what if the terror suspect turns out to be innocent?

And what torture regime in the history of the world has not tortured masses of innocents?

I have a friend, a black South African, who was tortured in Zimbabwe by Robert Mugabe's paranoid regime. I will call my friend Stephen. He is as good a man as I have met, humble and true. He told me that after three months of being tortured he no longer knew what he believed. He told me two men "worked" on him. One apologized and said he was doing it because he had no choice; the other didn't apologize at all. Maybe Stephen was this man's idea of a ticking bomb. I didn't ask Stephen what had been done to him, but briefly, in his eyes, I saw a wild liquid fear that reflected the horrible injury done to him in every way.

Before meeting Stephen I had gone to Robben Island, where Nelson Mandela was detained. The man who showed us around had been tortured and was scarcely sane. We entered the dormitory where he had been locked up each night, and he flung shut the metal door so that it clanged mightily in our ears. Most of us were looking the other way and jumped. "That is how they shut it," he cried. Painted in ghostly writing on the brick wall at the other end of the dormitory were the words HAPPY DAYS ARE HERE AGAIN.

Our guide gave us a full account of his torture. His limbs had been bound to his body with chains, then he had been lifted to a height of five feet and dropped onto a cement floor. Lifted and dropped, lifted and dropped. His hands had been tied behind his back. An Alsatian had savaged his genitals. Having told us this and more, he marched off, throwing his hands about and talking loudly. He broke into tears when saying good-bye.

It was after he told us of his torture that we swept past Mandela's cell. Of a size a prize animal might be kept in at a rural show, it was completely open to view. No privacy. It was from this bare place, surrounded by damaged people like our guide, that Mandela converted not only the other prisoners but also some of his guards to his belief in human dignity.

Stephen took me to his home. He had two small boys, about six and three, who had just been caught up in the excitement of the Cricket World Cup. We played backyard cricket. Stephen came out and played too. So there we were in the late golden glow of an African day, a smell of dust in the air. As an Australian male born after the Second World War, I could think of no greater image of boyhood innocence than a game of backyard cricket. But the man with whom I was playing this innocent game had been tortured. This wasn't an issue of race. His torturers, like Stephen, were black. The moral relativities of the twentieth century couldn't find a way around this one. That day I knew I could no longer deny the existence of evil.

I don't claim to be a wholly rational man, but who is? Anyone who says they can be detached about a subject like torture is fatally disconnected from what the great poet of the First World War trenches, Wilfred Owen, called "the eternal reciprocity of tears." Wilfred Owen considered such people cursed.

The arguments for torture, like so many of the arguments for war, are always presented as the work of superrealists— the sort who come to the fore in times of crisis when all illusions of human existence are swept away—but you would have to be naive or worse to believe torture can be conducted, as is now being argued, under controlled circumstances. As I understand it, the Inquisition was also conducted under controlled circumstances; the inquisitors were not allowed to draw blood, just break bones and pull limbs from sockets.

Torture is evil. Sanction the practice and it will assume the character of an institution, with those who do it best rising to positions of command.

In writing this essay I have tried to explain my beliefs in a personal way. I challenge those arguing for torture, in whatever form or circumstance, to do the same. Take us behind the walls of your proclamations. Show us who you really are. What makes you believe as you do? I challenge those people to put their opinions to one side and tell us a story about the reality of torture. Here's mine.

When I left South Africa, Stephen ran me to the airport. We had become close and talked a lot. Stephen had turned away from the use of violence as a political weapon during the apartheid years, having seen where it led. Instead he worked for peace. It was at the airport that he told me those few details of his torture.

We were standing at a desk awaiting service. I'd lost my ticket. All I had to get me back to Australia was a name on a piece of paper. South Africa is part first world, part third world, and you're never sure which part you're getting. The man with the piece of paper had been gone ten minutes when he reappeared in the distance. I was going to run over and grab him. Stephen looked at him and at me and said, "Trust him. It usually works."

It did. Stephen, a small man, is a moral mountain. I choose to be guided by him, and people like him.

As unimaginable as it may now seem, the issue of torture goes way beyond our time. The war against terror began as a moral crusade, a war against evil. Now our man-made moral universe is being reshaped, and with phenomenal speed. I am reminded of the words of the great Aboriginal leader Patrick Dodson, who said to me recently that he thought we were on the edge of a new dark age.

The arguments for torture haven't really changed since the Inquisition. What has changed is what's terrifying us and who we suspect its agents among us to be. What has changed is us.

Don't Forget

Thomas Lynch

from *Image*

An Irish American visits Tommy and Nora on the banks of the River Shannon.

I was the first of my people to return.

My great-grandfather Thomas Curry Lynch never returned to this house he was born in or ever saw his family here again. My grandfather Edward, proud to be Irish, nonetheless inherited the tribal scars of hunger and want, hardship and shame, and was prouder still to be American. He never made the trip. He worked in parcel post at the main post office in Detroit, wore a green tie on St. Patrick's Day, frequented the bars on Fenkell Avenue until he swore off drink when my father went to war, and spoke of Ireland as a poor old place that couldn't feed its own. And though he never had the brogue his parents brought with them and never knew this place except by name, he included in his prayers over Sunday dinners a blessing on his two unmarried cousins who lived together here then, "Tommy and Nora," whom he had never met, "on the banks of the River Shannon," which he had never seen, and always added, "Don't forget."

Bless us, O Lord, and these thy gifts
which we are about to receive from thy bounty.
Through Christ our Lord.
Amen.
And don't forget your cousins
Tommy and Nora Lynch
on the banks of the River Shannon.
Don't forget.

The powerful medicine of words remains, as Constantine Cavafy wrote:

Ideal and beloved voices
of those who are dead, or of those
who are lost to us like the dead.
Sometimes they speak to us in our dreams;
sometimes in thought the mind hears them.
And with their sound for a moment return
other sounds from the first poetry of our life—
like distant music that dies off in the night.

And this is how my grandfather's voice returns to me now— here in my fifties, and him dead now "with" forty years (in Moveen, life and time go "with" each other)—"like distant music that dies off in the night," like "the first poetry of our life."

Bless us, O Lord.
Tommy and Nora.
Banks of the Shannon.
Don't forget. Don't forget.

He is standing at the head of the dining room table in the brown brick bungalow with the green canvas awning on the porch overlooking Monte Vista Street, two blocks north of St. Francis de Sales on the corner of Fenkell Avenue in Detroit. It is any Sunday in the 1950s, and my father and my mother and my brothers, Dan and Pat and Tim, are there, and our baby sister, Mary Ellen, and Pop and Gramm Lynch and Aunt Marilyn and Uncle Mike, and we've been to Mass that morning at St. Columban's, where Father Kenny, a native of Galway, held forth in his flush-faced brogue about being "stingy with the Lord and the Lord'll be stingy with you," and we've had breakfast after Mass with the O'Haras—our mother's people, Nana and Uncle Pat and Aunt Pat and Aunt Sally Jean and Uncle Lou—and then we all piled in the car to drive from the suburbs into town to my father's parents' house for dinner. And my grandfather, Pop Lynch, is there at the head of the dining room table, near enough the age that I am now, the windows behind him, the crystal chandelier, all of us posing as in a Rockwell print—with the table and turkey and family gathered round—and he is blessing us and the food and giving thanks and telling us finally, "Don't forget" these people none of us has ever met, "Tommy and Nora Lynch on the banks of the River Shannon. Don't forget."

This was part of the first poetry of my life—the raised speech of blessing and remembrance, names of people and places far away, about whom and which we knew nothing but the sound of the names, the syllables. It was the repetition; it was the ritual, almost liturgical, tone of my grandfather's prayer that made the utterance memorable. Was it something he learned at his father's table—to pray for the family back in Ireland? It was his father, Thomas Lynch, who had left wherever the banks of the Shannon were and come to Jackson, Michigan, and painted new cell blocks in the prison and stripped Studebakers in an auto shop there. Was it the old bald man in the pictures with the grim missus in the high-necked blouse who first included in the grace before meals a remembrance of the people and the place he'd left behind and would never see again?

> Bless us, O Lord.
> Tommy and Nora.
> Banks of the Shannon.
> Don't forget.

When I arrived in 1970, I found the place as he had left it eighty years before, and the cousins we'd been praying for all my life. Tommy was holding back the barking dog in the yard. Nora was making her way to the gate, smiling and waving, all focus and calculation. They seemed to me like figures out of a Brueghel print: weathered, plain clothed, bright eyed, beckoning. Words made flesh—the childhood grace incarnate: *Tommy and Nora. Don't forget.* It was wintry and windy and gray, the first Tuesday morning of the first February of the 1970s. I was twenty-one.

"Go on, boy. That's your people now," the taximan who'd brought me from Shannon said. I paid him and thanked him and grabbed my bag.

I've been coming and going here ever since.

Obedient unto Death

Margaret Roche Macey

from *America*

What faithfulness to a vow cost Father Paul Dent.

In the summer of 1975, I met Paul Dent, SJ. I was passing through Chicago and stopped to visit a friend who was spending the summer at Loyola University. He invited me to stay for dinner, and we decided to go to a late-afternoon Mass before we ate.

The Mass was held in the basement of a Jesuit residence, where some rows of folding chairs had been set up under a low ceiling and asbestos-wrapped pipes. I was looking forward to the kind of informal celebration I had learned to expect from the Jesuits: relaxed but (I hate now to put quotes around it) "meaningful." So I was amazed and disappointed when in walked a skinny old man with a crew cut, wearing every sort of vestment permissible and carrying a chalice covered by an old-fashioned liturgical veil.

Before he began, he announced that he would say the Mass of the Sacred Heart, which was the Mass he always said to celebrate "how Jesus loved us with the human heart that Mary gave him." By this time he had begun to remind me of the priests of my childhood. I found myself slipping into that gear and decided to enjoy the celebration on a nostalgic level, if nothing else. Nonetheless I was impatient when, after reading the Gospel, he asked us to sit for a homily. But then the experience began to change into something altogether different.

The priest told us his name and said that this was to be his last Mass at Loyola; he was leaving in the morning to return to India. He had joined the Jesuits because he felt called to the missions in India; he had, in fact, studied theology and been ordained there. But not long after he arrived in Patna, a city in northeast India, he was diagnosed with a brain tumor and sent back to Chicago for surgery. "Get well and come back soon" had been written on a banner for his farewell dinner.

The success of the surgery was questionable, however, and the doctors suggested that he remain in Chicago for observation. After a year, his condition was unchanged, so he petitioned his provincial superior for permission to return to the missions. This was denied for reasons of health. He petitioned again the following year, and again the one after that. This continued until he heard that the provincial himself was dying. Father Dent managed to get in to see him and again asked that he be allowed to return to his people in India. Again he was told to wait another year. And another year. Each new provincial responded in the same way. As crazy as it sounds, this went on for what must have been over thirty years. And still he waited.

It is hard to say why this story was so powerful for me. I sat on that folding chair in the basement listening and watching a man grow old so far away from the center of his life. He never told us what he had done for all those years in Chicago. I hope it had some value for others. But from what he said that afternoon, it seemed that for him, on some essential level, time had pretty much stood still. The life he had always planned had ended just months after it had begun.

As a product of the 1960s, I knew what I would have done, and what I thought he should have done. These provincials had obviously been wrong. They were keeping him from responding to a genuine need and to his real calling. In India, his life of service, for however long, would have had meaning. Follow God, not the political structure of bureaucrats—even Jesuit bureaucrats.

And then I suddenly realized: this man had been obedient for longer than I had been alive. But what a stupid, old-fashioned, useless virtue. Hadn't obedience slipped away somewhere around seventh grade or during the Second Vatican Council? Hadn't we grown beyond it? God gave us reason, simple common sense, and we were crazy to surrender that. Yet blind obedience was just such surrender.

The ultimate irony in his story was that his doctors had recently told him that he did in fact have inoperable brain cancer; and in a totally irrational reaction, his province had agreed to send him to India to die. But even that was not simple. He could not get a visa, so he was flying to Turkey in hopes that he would somehow be allowed into India through Pakistan. Get well and come back soon.

He spoke simply, softly, without the slightest hint of drama. Yet by the time he had finished, many of us sitting there had tears on our faces. What moved us was not the waste of a life or the impending death of an old man. What so caught us, I think, was a recognition that in that simple old man was a force that was palpably real and totally beyond us.

As moved as I had been by his homily, the strongest part of my encounter with Father Dent was yet to come. As we all stood during the consecration of the Mass, this priest raised the Host and said, "This is my body, which will be given up for you." And he held the elevated wafer there, looking at it.

I wasn't keeping track of the time, but he stood there just looking at that Host for probably sixty, maybe ninety, seconds. A ridiculous length of time. But watching him look at it, I got just a glimpse of the implication of those words. This is my body, which will be given. This is my life, which will be spent, used up, thrown away—not in glory, but in useless, meaningless sacrifice. For that period of time, no one else, nothing else, existed for him except that Host, and in his face I saw the recognition of what that reality meant. He too had been obedient even unto death.

I thought then of the apostles, who had run away, who had been unwilling not only to follow but also to watch as Jesus paid the price. And standing there in that basement in Chicago, I found myself praying for the strength to be faithful to the insight of that moment, to be willing to witness, in a concentrated ninety-second period, to the pain that living a life centered on something beyond reason would exact. Again in tears, I finally looked away.

I received communion that day from the hands of Father Dent. In some way, I participated in his sacrifice.

After Mass, I saw him walking outside and went to meet him. I don't remember at all what I said to him, but I remember that he talked again, in a very simple way, about the Sacred Heart and the great love God has for us. He urged me to say the prayer that he constantly prayed: "Lord, Jesus, I love you with all my heart." And he asked my name and told me that he would pray for me.

That was thirty years ago this past summer. In daily life, especially in today's world of religious fundamentalism, I have not at all changed my view that rules can at times function mainly as a guide, and that we cannot hand over our reason—our greatest gift—to blind forces. Vows are taken and meant to be kept. But on some level, we are responsible for our lives, and even God does not want us to abandon our own good or that of others.

And yet, thirty years later, I still think of Father Dent. I do not know if he ever made it to India or how long he lived. But I don't think I have ever been near anyone who was closer to God than he was. And I know that somehow, in the total irrationality of his life, he touched a tremendous truth.

Note: Paul Dent, SJ, died in Patna, India, in 1980, at age seventy-nine.

Going to Chimayó

Don Haynes

from *Portland Magazine*

She said, "I need a miracle." And that's what happened.

My sister calls in the evening. Her husband is near death. He's not expected to pull through. We start praying. Everyone starts praying.

I fly to New Mexico to be with her. We drive to the hospital.

"This is where Bob lives," she says.

We walk into his ward. He lies on his back. He looks serene, but it is the serenity of statuary, empty and vacant. Gail catches his beard with both hands. Pulls his face against hers. Calls him. Demands that he look at her. *Hear me!* Then she begins to spoon small amounts of cantaloupe into his mouth.

"I get up early," she tells me, "and pray. Scripture reading. I'm calm. I can handle things. Then I go to see him and I cry. I don't stop. If I'm there for three hours, I cry for three hours."

We go eat, and for the first time we begin to deal with the situation. It is an odd conversation. We both accept the fiction that Bob will recover. At the same time we begin to plan a future for her without him. She will return to school, complete her degree, go on for a master's degree . . .

We enter the cathedral in Santa Fe, the one Willa Cather wrote about in *Death Comes for the Archbishop*. It is a beautiful church. Clean. Orderly. Oriented toward the tourist trade. Just inside the main doors is a large gift shop doing terrific business. Inside the church a man is vacuuming the floor, going up and down the aisles, ignoring those who are there to pray.

"There's a place near here where there are miracles," says my sister. "I want to go there. I want to go to Chimayó." We go to Chimayó.

Chimayó is thirty miles northeast of Santa Fe. The church is old. Sticking out of the white stucco, in stark contrast to its glare, are stubs of dark rafters. As we enter the church, an old woman in a black dress steps out from the side.

"I need a miracle," my sister says, a catch in her voice.

"Go ask," the old woman says.

We descend three steps into the church. They are hollowed out by centuries of feet. The church is small and narrow. The statues are nearly grotesque, looking almost like marionettes from some garish sideshow. So too the stations of the cross. This church offers nothing to the tourist. It exists on its own raw terms.

People are coming through a door to the left of the altar. I walk through it into a room covered floor to ceiling with pictures of Jesus. All kinds of images. Smiling. Frowning. Serious. Laughing. Here and there a testimonial, some printed, some handwritten. In the far corner of the room crutches and canes lean in a loose bundle against the wall.

There's a small low door in another corner, and I watch three people emerge from it, stooping as they come. My sister stoops and goes through the door. I follow. Another room, this one smaller still. The same mixture of pictures of Jesus and testimonials. The floor slopes to the center of the room where there is a hole, a foot or so across, with dirt in it. A family comes in behind us. Immediately they kneel around the hole. One of them begins putting dirt in the hands of the rest. My sister kneels and holds out both hands, and a woman fills her hands with the dirt. The woman offers me dirt. I wash my hands with it. It leaves a silky feel. The family rises and walks out. My sister continues to kneel in prayer.

On the way home my sister tells me that during Holy Week many people walk the thirty miles from Santa Fe to Chimayó. People set up tables with water and food along the road to feed the pilgrims.

The next day, late in the afternoon, as we do errands and such, my sister is possessed of a sudden impatience, a burning need to get back to the hospital and see her husband, and she drives away hurriedly. I look at the mountains.

My sister is supposed to return at five. Six o'clock comes and goes. So does seven. At last the phone rings. It is my sister: the miracle has happened. Her husband is healed.

The doctors are astonished. They keep looking for some organic cause for his healing. They find none. Yesterday they were preparing to remove the tube through which he was taking nourishment. Now he is talking to them.

We learn that at about the time we were in Chimayó, a cleaning woman came into Bob's room. As was her custom, she sang hymns as she cleaned. She sang "Amazing Grace," and suddenly Bob sang too.

Months later, my brother-in-law is fully recovered, fully healed. He remembers nothing of what happened to him.

Common sense tells me there must be some other explanation than a miracle. I long for some scientific tidiness. Something predictable. Comfortable. Controllable. Not this raw, ragged, ugly, unfinished, irrational rupture in causality. Not a God who answers prayers.

Contributors

John L. Allen Jr. is the Vatican writer for the *National Catholic Reporter*. His weekly column, "The Word from Rome," is pretty much a must for Catholic readers. He is also the author of *Cardinal Ratzinger: The Vatican's Enforcer of the Faith* and *Conclave: The Politics, Personalities, and Process of the Next Papal Election.*

Clare Ansberry is the Pittsburgh bureau chief for the *Wall Street Journal* and author of *The Women of Troy Hill: The Back-Fence Virtues of Faith and Friendship.*

Pedro Arrupe, SJ, (1907–91) served as the twenty-eighth superior general of the Society of Jesus, from 1965 to 1983.

Clare Asquith, an English native, is the author of *Shadowplay: The Hidden Beliefs and Coded Politics of William Shakespeare,* from which her essay here is drawn. It appeared first in the admirable American magazine *Commonweal.*

Douglas Beaumont teaches at Southern Evangelical Seminary and Bible College. He is one of the contributors to the philosophy blog Tu Quoque (http://tuquoque.blogspot .com/), where he describes himself as "a professor of apologetics, ordained minister, armchair philosopher, backseat theologian, and all around righteous dude."

Pope Benedict XVI, the former Cardinal Joseph Ratzinger, was elected the 265th pope of the Roman Catholic Church on April 19, 2005. He is the author of many books, among them *The Spirit of the Liturgy; God Is Near Us: The Eucharist, the Heart of Life;* and *Truth and Tolerance: Christian Belief and World Religions.*

George Coyne, SJ, is director of the Vatican Observatory, an adjunct professor of astronomy at the University of Arizona, and a riveting guy—he did a spectrophotometric study of the moon to earn his doctorate from Georgetown University in 1962 and has had a comet named after him.

Kevin Cullen is a reporter for the *Boston Globe.* He has been that newspaper's law enforcement, legal, and city reporter; London and Dublin bureau chief; and European correspondent. Among the honors his work has earned are the Livingston Award for local reporting and an Overseas Press Club Award for his coverage of the war in Northern Ireland.

Brian Doyle edited the first three volumes of the annual Best Catholic Writing anthology (2004, 2005, 2006). He is the editor of *Portland Magazine* at the University of Portland, in Oregon, and is the author most recently of *The Wet Engine: Exploring the Mad Wild Miracle of the Heart* and *The Grail,* about a year in the life of an Oregon vineyard. His essay collection *Leaping: Revelations and Epiphanies* was published by Loyola Press in 2003.

Robert Ellsberg is editor in chief of Orbis Books. He was a member of the Catholic Worker community in New York from 1975 to 1980. His latest book is *Blessed among All Women: Women Saints, Prophets, and Witnesses for Our Time.*

Martin Flanagan is an award-winning writer for the *Age* newspaper in Melbourne, Australia, and director of One

Day Hill Publishers in the Lucky Country. His many books include *The Game in Time of War* and, most recently, *The Line,* about his father's prisoner-of-war experiences during the Second World War. Martin is at work on a book about the great Australian football player and social activist Michael Long.

Ron Hansen is a professor of literature at Santa Clara University, in California, and the author of many books, among them the novels *The Assassination of Jesse James by the Coward Robert Ford, Mariette in Ecstasy, Atticus,* and *Hitler's Niece.* His most recent book is *Isn't It Romantic?: An Entertainment.*

David Bentley Hart is an Orthodox theologian who has taught at the University of Virginia; the University of St. Thomas, in St. Paul, Minnesota; Duke Divinity School; and Loyola College in Maryland. He is the author of *The Beauty of the Infinite: The Aesthetics of Christian Truth* and *The Doors of the Sea: Where Was God in the Tsunami?*

Don Haynes is a writer and photographer in Klamath Falls, Oregon.

Seamus Heaney, who won the Nobel Prize for Literature in 1995, is the author of many books of poems, among them *Station Island, The Haw Lantern, The Spirit Level,* and *District and Circle.* He has for many years been a ferocious advocate for, as he said in his Nobel lecture, "poetry's power to do the thing which always is and always will be to poetry's credit: the power to persuade that vulnerable part of our conscious-ness of its rightness in spite of the evidence of wrongness all around it, the power to remind us that we are hunters and gatherers of values, that our very solitudes and distresses are creditable, insofar as they, too, are an earnest of our veritable human being."

Joe Hoover, SJ, is a scholastic who is in his third year of a three-year philosophy program at Loyola University Chicago. He is a native of Omaha, Nebraska.

John Kavanaugh, SJ, is professor of philosophy and director of ethics across the curriculum at St. Louis University. He writes the "Ethics Notebook" column in *America* magazine.

Robert P. Lockwood, former president and publisher of *Our Sunday Visitor,* is director of communications for the Diocese of Pittsburgh. Among his books is *A Faith for Grown-Ups: A Midlife Conversation about What Really Matters.*

Thomas Lynch is a poet and an essayist whose books include *Skating with Heather Grace; The Undertaking: Life Studies from the Dismal Trade,* which won an American Book Award and was a finalist for the National Book Award; *Still Life in Milford;* and *Bodies in Motion and at Rest: On Metaphor and Mortality.* Lynch lives in Milford, Michigan, where he works as a funeral director. The essay in this anthology is drawn from his book *Booking Passage: We Irish and Americans* which, if you are American of Irish ancestry, you have to read.

Margaret Roche Macey is a retired teacher and writer who lives in upstate New York.

Frank Moan, SJ, is in residence at Holy Name Rectory, Camden, New Jersey.

Peggy Noonan is a contributing editor of the *Wall Street Journal* and author of, among other books, *What I Saw at the*

Revolution: A Political Life in the Reagan Era and *John Paul the Great: Remembering a Spiritual Father.* She famously served as assistant to Reagan from 1984 to 1986 and as chief speech-writer for George H. W. Bush when he ran for the presidency in 1988.

Mary Oliver, one of the coolest poets in this sweet blue world, has won the National Book Award and the Pulitzer Prize for her work, among many honors. She is the author of many books, including *American Primitive, White Pine, Owls and Other Fantasies, Why I Wake Early,* and *Blue Iris.* She lives in Massachusetts.

Sandra Scofield is the author of seven novels, among them *A Chance to See Egypt* and *Plain Seeing.* Her most recent book is *Occasions of Sin,* a memoir. She lives in Montana.

Colm Tóibín is the author of many books of fiction and nonfiction, among them the novels *The Blackwater Lightship* and *The Master.* Among his nonfiction works are *Homage to Barcelona, The Sign of the Cross: Travels in Catholic Europe,* and *Lady Gregory's Toothbrush.*

Amy Welborn is the keeper and firestarter of the blog Open Book (http://amywelborn.typepad.com/openbook) and author of several books, including *De-coding Da Vinci: The Facts behind the Fiction of The Da Vinci Code* and the *Prove It!* series of booklets about Catholicism.

Jonathan Yardley is a book critic and columnist for the *Washington Post.* He is the author of *Ring: A Biography of Ring Lardner* and *Misfit: The Strange Life of Frederick Exley.* Yardley received the Pulitzer Prize for Criticism in 1981.

Acknowledgments

"We Want God!" by Peggy Noonan. Originally published in the *Wall Street Journal,* April 7, 2005. Copyright © 2005 by Dow Jones and Company. All rights reserved. Reprinted with permission of the *Wall Street Journal.*

"Five Years with Dorothy Day" by Robert Ellsberg. Originally published in *America,* November 21, 2005. Copyright © 2005. All rights reserved. Reprinted with permission of America Press. For subscription information, visit www .americamagazine.org.

"It Is Not Power, but Love That Redeems Us!" by Pope Benedict XVI. From the homily at his inauguration Mass, April 24, 2005.

"Six Recognitions of the Lord" by Mary Oliver. Originally published in *Shenandoah* (Spring/Summer 2005). Copyright © 2005 by Mary Oliver. All rights reserved. Reprinted with permission of the author.

"Are Young Catholics Embracing Orthodoxy?" by Amy Welborn and Others. Originally published at Open Book, http://amywelborn.typepad.com/openbook, March 3, 2005. Copyright © 2005 by Amy Welborn. All rights reserved. Reprinted with permission of the author.

"Sister Rosemarie Wants You" by Clare Ansberry. Originally published in the *Wall Street Journal,* December 17, 2005.

George Coyne. All rights reserved. Reprinted with permission of the *Tablet* (www.thetablet.co.uk).

"The Writer Who Was Full of Grace" by Jonathan Yardley. Originally published in the *Washington Post,* July 6, 2005. Copyright © 2005 by Jonathan Yardley. All rights reserved. Reprinted with permission of the *Washington Post.*

"Confirmation Day" by Seamus Heaney. Originally published in *Agni* 61. Copyright © 2005 by Seamus Heaney. All rights reserved. Reprinted with permission of the author.

"The Existence of Chuck Norris" by Douglas Beaumont. Originally published at Tu Quoque, http://tuquoque .blogspot.com/, February 10, 2006. Copyright © 2006 by Douglas Beaumont. All rights reserved. Reprinted with permission of the author.

"Tremors of Doubt" by David Bentley Hart. Originally published in the *Wall Street Journal,* December 31, 2004. Copyright © 2004 by Dow Jones and Company. All rights reserved. Reprinted with permission of the *Wall Street Journal.*

"Merry Sunshine" by Joe Hoover. Copyright © 2005 by Joe Hoover. All rights reserved. Reprinted with permission of the author.

"Self-Hating Humanity?" by John F. Kavanaugh. Originally published in *America,* March 28, 2005. Copyright © 2005. All rights reserved. Reprinted with permission of America Press. For subscription information, visit www .americamagazine.org.

Send us the best Catholic writing you've read

Loyola Press's Best Catholic Writing is an annual collection, and all manner of written work concerning Catholic life is eligible for inclusion in the next volume, *The Best Catholic Writing 2007*. We will consider all writing that is true, remarkable, and Catholic-minded in the largest possible sense.

Please send any articles, essays, poems, short stories, plays, speeches, sermons, elegies, eulogies, monologues, rants, raves, etc., that have been written or published in 2005 or 2006. We will also consider book excerpts and yet-to-be-published writings.

Send nominated entries by fax, e-mail attachment, or snail mail to

Jim Manney
Loyola Press
3441 North Ashland Avenue
Chicago, IL 60657
E-mail: manney@loyolapress.com
Fax: (734) 663-8739

A Special Invitation
from Loyola Press

Loyola Press invites you to become one of our Loyola Press Advisors! Join our unique online community of people willing to share with us their thoughts and ideas about Catholic life and faith. By sharing your perspective, you will help us improve our books and serve the greater Catholic community.

From time to time, registered advisors are invited to participate in online surveys and discussion groups. Most surveys will take less than ten minutes to complete. Loyola Press will recognize your time and efforts with gift certificates and prizes. Your personal information will be held in strict confidence. Your participation will be for research purposes only, and at no time will we try to sell you anything.

Please consider this opportunity to help Loyola Press improve our products and better serve you and the Catholic community. To learn more or to join, visit **www.SpiritedTalk .org** and register today.

—The Loyola Press Advisory Team

Also available in the Best Catholic Writing series

The Best Catholic Writing 2005
Edited by Brian Doyle
0-8294-2088-6 · $14.95
Paperback · 256 pages

The admired Best Catholic Writing series continues with contributions from R. Scott Appleby, Kenneth L. Woodward, Ron Hansen, James Martin, SJ, and twenty-four other essayists, poets, novelists, scholars, and journalists. The selections deal with pressing public questions, spiritual issues, and lively Catholic personalities.

The Best Catholic Writing 2004
Edited by Brian Doyle
0-8294-1729-X · $14.95
Paperback · 248 pages

This first of its kind collection of best Catholic writing features timely, thought-provoking works from the brightest voices on Catholic issues. Featured writers include Alice McDermott, Andrew Greeley, Paul Elie, Kathleen Norris, and many more.

*Available at your favorite bookstore or call **800.621.1008** or visit **www.loyolabooks.org** to order.*